fire

Junkers 88

The Sky Suspended

This book is for
JACK and SUSAN

THE SKY
SUSPENDED

BY

DREW MIDDLETON

Their shoulders held the sky suspended,
They stood, and earth's foundations stay . . .

—A. E. HOUSMAN,
"Epitaph on an Army of Mercenaries"

LONGMANS, GREEN AND CO.

NEW YORK · LONDON · TORONTO
1960

LONGMANS, GREEN AND CO., INC.
119 WEST 40TH STREET, NEW YORK 18

LONGMANS, GREEN AND CO., LTD.
6 & 7 CLIFFORD STREET, LONDON W 1

LONGMANS, GREEN AND CO.
20 CRANFIELD ROAD, TORONTO 16

87249

THE SKY SUSPENDED

COPYRIGHT © 1960
BY
DREW MIDDLETON

ALL RIGHTS RESERVED, INCLUDING THE RIGHT TO REPRODUCE
THIS BOOK, OR ANY PORTION THEREOF, IN ANY FORM

PUBLISHED SIMULTANEOUSLY IN THE DOMINION OF CANADA BY
LONGMANS, GREEN AND CO., TORONTO

FIRST EDITION

LIBRARY OF CONGRESS CATALOG CARD NUMBER: 60–15277

Printed in the United States of America

INTRODUCTION

This book is in part payment of a debt which I, in common with all who love freedom, owe the pilots of Fighter Command. To a great degree this is their story. It is also the story of the pilots and air crews of the Luftwaffe, brave and steadfast men, terribly mishandled and serving an odious tyranny. Finally it is a story of the ordinary men and women of the United Kingdom. The story of 1940 cannot be confined to the battle in the air. The British national effort included popular resistance to the bombing of London and the provincial cities as well as the daylight battle over southeast England. Unless we see the scene as a whole, we cannot grasp the significance of those events of twenty years ago.

So many good books have been written about various aspects of the war in 1940 that it would be impossible to list them all. For the day-to-day conduct of operations I have relied upon *The Defence of the United Kingdom* of the United Kingdom Military Series. Written by Basil Collier, this is surely one of the finest records of its type. No historian will be able to write about the war without it. Volume I of *The Royal Air Force, 1939–1945* by Denis Richards contains the best short account of the Battle of

INTRODUCTION

Britain that I have read. As the reader will learn, I have supplemented these accounts with notes from my own diary of the period and with the log of 85 Squadron. Adolf Galland's *The First and the Last* is the best German record on the operational level. Captured German documents, particularly the War Diaries of the Naval Staff and the minutes of Hitler's conferences with the naval commanders, provide an intimate picture of the German High Command during the invasion period. *Hitler as War Lord* by General Halder is a professional soldier's picture of his terrible chieftain. The best book written in the West about the invasion is Peter Fleming's *Invasion 1940*, which appeared in the United States as *Operation Sea Lion*. On the bombing of London there is, in addition to the numerous local histories and the newspaper files, *The Blitz* by Constantine Fitz Gibbon, a clear and moving story of London's trial. Finally I must acknowledge my debt, as every writer about the period must do, to Sir Winston Churchill's *The Second World War*.

To William H. Stoneman, my friend and companion then as now, the book and I owe a great deal.

D.M.

London
April 8, 1960

Chapter I

The news had been bad for a week. The national euphoria arising from the deliverance at Dunkirk had been replaced by gloom, the consequence of a succession of terrible reverses. The evacuation might have been a great feat of arms, although the Prime Minister was careful to tell the nation that wars are not won by evacuations, but how unimportant it appeared against the catastrophes that now overtook the Allied cause. The illusions, the wishful thoughts, were being stripped from the British one by one, leaving them almost naked before the storm that rolled through Europe.

It was a week of long, hot, sunny days and cool scented nights. In France, where the last divisions of the British Expeditionary Force tried to plug the holes torn in the French line, men cursed the wide blue sky for the German bombers it encouraged. In London people thought the fine spell unsuitable to the terrible events. Such weather reminded them of other Junes, of the Derby, Wimbledon and Ascot, of cricket on village greens, ribald excursions from London's East End to Southend, of peaceful afternoons on the river. Rain and a cold wind would have suited the temper that week in the London of June, 1940.

[1]

June 10 had been a day of disaster. The German Sixth Army, part of the army group commanded by Colonel General Gerd von Rundstedt, had smashed from the Somme to the Seine in five days and the panzers rumbled into Vernon, just over forty miles west of Paris. In the capital they were burning government documents. The government, headed by Paul Reynaud, was preparing to leave for Tours. On the extreme left of the Allied line, the 51st Highland Division, which had been fighting with the French Tenth Army, found itself cut off at Saint-Valéry. The hopes that the French army, which, in one of the clichés of the day, had been called "the finest standing army in the world," would rally and halt the Germans were baseless. The panzers punched holes in the French line almost at will. That day, too, Mussolini carried Italy into the war. This opened a new front in the southeast of France. The British had no high regard for the Italian forces but they realized that their addition to the great weight of the German onslaught might be decisive for France.

To the people of Britain the subsequent words of Franklin Roosevelt at the University of Virginia were little comfort. Certainly Italy had stabbed France in the back. Surely it was correct of the President to cite the danger to "our" institutions. It was interesting but not particularly helpful to know that the President thought that "the whole of our sympathies" lay with the embattled Allies. The United States was infinitely more remote from Britain in 1940 than it is in 1960. If the President understood what was happening, people said, he understood that something more than sympathy was necessary to halt the Germans.

On June 14 the Germans entered Paris. In France this was only one more shock of the many endured thus far. In Le Mans a weeping woman was asked if she wept for Paris. "No, monsieur, for France."

For the British, however, the fall of Paris was a grievous emotional shock. There were then in Britain hundreds of thousands of men who had fought and bled to prevent a German army's reaching Paris a generation before. To them and to millions of their countrymen Paris had a mystique; this welcoming enchantress, half-wanton, half-priestess, who satiated the senses and excited the mind. Men and women stood by their windows staring unseeing at the sunlit, busy streets. In the mind's eye they saw the little bistro off the Avenue de l'Opéra, the great sweep of the Champs-Elysées on a spring day, all the memories that gave Paris a special quality in their eyes. For many it was the worst moment of a war that was to have many bad ones.

There was little to comfort the British. A study of the citations for medals published in the *Times* would disclose, in somewhat guarded fashion, just how gallantly the BEF had fought in the long retreat and at Boulogne, Calais and Dunkirk. There was some solace in the obvious and growing unity of the country. The disappearance of *Action*, the weekly publication of Sir Oswald Mosley's fascist organization, was welcome. But what were these against the news from France? Pétain had become head of the government and General Maxime Weygand was his deputy. We heard the news in a little village in Brittany, Saint-Aubin d'Aubigny.

"The French are chucking it," an officer said. "We're heading for Brest tomorrow. They've promised to give us time to go. I hope to God they do. There's part of an armored division somewhere to the northeast. Well, there it is."

It was a quiet night. Sometimes we could hear the rumble of artillery to the north. The priest and the chief of police were good to us. They were old soldiers.

The next day we moved westward toward Brest and the second, lesser-known evacuation. The countryside was sweet and smiling, untouched as yet by war, as quiet as a painted landscape. When the British reached Brest the troops marched down to the docks and, as they always do, children ran out to march beside them. Their fathers and mothers ran after them, caught them, and slapped them. No one wanted to have anything to do with the British. So in contempt and bitterness on both sides the campaign ended. To watch a country you have known and loved disintegrate morally and physically is a traumatic experience. Those who saw it had need of hope.

When the destroyer slipped out of the harbor in the dusk, an elderly captain of artillery said he hoped they would give him a gun again so he could kill a few Germans. Everyone knew the killing would be done in England. For these older men, officers in the first war and complacent, comfortable householders in the long weekend between the wars, the hour of reckoning had arrived.

When we returned on the night of the 17th, London, the silly inconsequential London of gay restaurants and hotel bars that never quite disappeared in the war, was full of rumors. The Germans were offering an alliance against the Russians. . . . Pétain was a sly old boy who meant to fight on in Africa and was simply playing for time. . . . They say the German generals are worried by their losses. . . . They say the Jerries are running short of oil. . . . They say the Russians have told the Germans to get out of Poland. . . . They say, they say.

The government had issued a curious statement which said in part "at a time like the present it is natural that there should be baseless and ill-informed rumors of peace proposals and negotiations. It cannot be too clearly and definitely stated that Great Britain is firmly and resolutely determined to continue the struggle until victory has been won." The statement with its claim that Germany was consuming her resources on "a reckless scale" and its defensive tone belonged to an earlier period of the war, the period of uncertainty and frustration. Such words were ill attuned to the nobler leadership now coming from Downing Street.

June 17 had been a busy day at Downing Street where Mr. Churchill, in his own words, was "getting on with the war." That day the Prime Minister had reviewed the disposition of the fleet: *Repulse* and *Renown* at Scapa Flow, *Nelson* and *Rodney* and *Valiant* at Rosyth to cover "the Island," and *Hood* and *Ark Royal* steaming to join *Reso-*

lution to observe the French fleet. "If we have to quit Gibraltar," Mr. Churchill wrote to the First Lord of the Admiralty, "we must immediately take the Canaries, which will serve as a very good base to control the western entrance to the Mediterranean."

The news that had flowed into Downing Street was almost uniformly bad. The French had begun armistice negotiations with the Germans in Madrid. That day, also, they brought to the Prime Minister the news that Latvia and Estonia had been occupied by the Red army. Mr. Churchill brooded over the news for a bit and then turned to a speech he was composing. There was only one hopeful development. A young, virtually unknown French brigadier general, one Charles de Gaulle, had landed in England to carry on the fight for the honor of France.

June 18 was warm and sunny. But the mood of the House of Commons, assembling to listen to a speech by the Prime Minister, was gloomy. France gone. The Italians in. The Middle East in danger. Warm words but little else from Washington. Those who pondered the terrible dangers thought harshly of those who had put the country in such straits.

The short, thick figure at the dispatch box had been thinking too. Now, in the supreme crisis, at the opening of his speech Mr. Churchill called for unity. To indict those who had been responsible in the past would be "a foolish and pernicious process." Rather, "let each man search his conscience." The strong voice rose. "Of this I am quite sure"—he pronounced it "shu-ah"—"that if we open a quarrel between the past and the present, we shall find we have lost the future." The government intended to stand together, govern the country, and fight the war.

Now that the French were defeated, the people of Britain and their representatives "in Commons assembled" were thinking of invasion. Winston Churchill did not avoid the topic. But perhaps to keep other nerves steady —there was nothing wrong with his own—he referred to the prospect obliquely as though he were considering some interesting military problem that might be a subject for intellectual exercise rather than a terrifying and immediate event. Invasion, he pointed out, would "require the transportation across the sea of hostile armies on a very large scale and after they had been so transported they would have to be continually maintained with all the masses of munitions and supplies which are required for continuous battle—as continuous battle it will surely be."

The House relaxed slightly. This sounded confident, as though the government knew its mind.

For those who were downcast over the entry of Italy into the war the Prime Minister offered laughter. The British had been told, Mr. Churchill said smoothly, that the Italian navy was to emerge from the Mediterranean and gain superiority in the Atlantic.

"If they seriously intend it, I shall only say that we shall be delighted to offer Signor Mussolini a free and safe-guarded passage through the Straits of Gibraltar in order that he may play the part to which he aspires." Here a ripple of laughter. "There is a general curiosity in the British fleet to find out whether the Italians are up to the level they were at in the last war or whether they have fallen off at all." Not perhaps much of a joke, but enough to reassure the worriers. This was defiance with a smile.

The thick, strong voice rolled on; slurring some words, mispronouncing others. Gradually it assumed a full-blooded toughness; this was a trumpet call to encourage the brave and rally the fainthearted as much as a declaration of policy. Noble passages alternated with blunt warnings anyone could understand. "Remember, the enemy is crafty and there is no dirty trick he will not do." This was the time when most military men thought that in the event of invasion Germany would use a mass of parachutists. But there was the Royal Air Force and "we believe ourselves possessed of the capacity to continue the war in the air under better conditions than we have ever experienced before." Not for the last time, the Prime Minister directed the country's attention to those who would do the fighting in the air:

"I look forward confidently to the exploits of our fighter pilots—these splendid men, this brilliant youth—who will have the glory of saving their native land, their island home, and all they love, from the most deadly of all attacks."

It was very quiet in the House now. In the press gallery men leaned forward to catch every word. The Commons followed Mr. Churchill as though mesmerized. In those days everyone in London felt he was living through one of the great moments of history; here was history in the grand manner, this was Pitt at the Guildhall, Lincoln at Gettysburg. Now the Prime Minister spoke of the "severity of the ordeal" that lay ahead. His voice rising he declared, "I believe our countrymen will show themselves capable of standing up to it, like the brave men of Barcelona." There was a burst of cheering from the Labour benches. Here was a Conservative prime minister paying tribute to those Spanish Republicans whose lost cause was so dear to British socialism.

Almost offhandedly the Prime Minister disclosed that "our professional advisers of the three Services unitedly advise that we should carry on the war, and that there are good and reasonable hopes of victory." But how far away victory seemed that afternoon. Yet in the enchantment of that speech it seemed a reasonable, almost a logical consequence of the Prime Minister's words. Even in the debris of defeat Mr. Churchill found reasons for cheer, reasons that would not have stood up to a minute's examination in less parlous times. "If invasion has become more imminent, as no doubt it has, we, relieved from the task of maintaining a large army in France, have far larger and more efficient forces to meet it." The effrontery, the sublime confidence of this attempt to transform a stunning defeat into a positive advantage was dazzling then, it is remarkable even today.

"Therefore, in casting up this dread balance sheet and contemplating our dangers with a disillusioned eye I see great reason for intense vigilance and exertion, but none whatever for panic or despair." He had the House now. There was a swelling chorus of "Hear, hear." The gloom had lifted. The atmosphere was almost gay as he entered his peroration.

The French would be throwing away much if they failed to continue the war, but whatever happened "we in this island and in the British Empire will never lose our sense of comradeship with the French people."

Now came the supreme defiance from the leader of a country fighting alone against an apparently invincible army, an undefeated air force, and the greatest submarine fleet the world had ever seen.

"We abate nothing of our just demands; not one jot or tittle do we recede. Czechs, Poles, Norwegians, Dutch, Belgians have joined their causes to our own. All these shall be restored." No one at that moment wondered how. The magic of words was enough. His tone firm, but his manner almost discursive, Mr. Churchill turned to his last sentences:

"What General Weygand called the Battle of France is over. I expect that the Battle of Britain is about to begin. Upon this battle depends the survival of Christian civilization. Upon it depends our own British life, and the long continuity of our institutions and our Empire. The whole fury and might of the enemy must very soon be turned upon us. Hitler knows that he will have to break us in this island or lose the war. If we can stand up to him, all Europe may be free and the life of the world may move into broad, sunlit uplands. But if we fail,

[10]

then the whole world, including the United States, including all that we have known and cared for, will sink into the abyss of a new Dark Age made more sinister, and perhaps more protracted, by the lights of perverted science. Let us therefore brace ourselves to our duties, and so bear ourselves that, if the British Empire and its Commonwealth last for a thousand years, men will still say 'This was their finest hour.'"

There was a brief silence. Then came a steady roar of cheering. On the benches MP's turned to their neighbors and nodded their heads; this was the challenge, here was their duty. Light and strength were in the air. Somehow from the recesses of the British spirit the challenge was to be met, the duty done. I felt a buoyant emotion that banished all I had seen and heard in France in the preceding six weeks. Somehow these incredible people were going to do it. I felt great gratitude for being there that day, confidence in the future. When I emerged into the street the sunshine seemed brighter.

That night he broadcast the speech to the nation.

Families gathered around their radios. It was June and warm, so many sat in the dusk leaving the blackout curtains undrawn—in June of 1940 this did not seem so important, later that year it became hideously important —and listened. In the pubs men paused with a pint of beer in their hands as the barmaid turned up the volume. People heard it in shipyards and factories, in lonely farmhouses. In the camps where the army licked its wounds, on the great ships rocking in the northern mists, in the messes on the airfields where the pilots waited, they listened.

When it was over people looked up at the quiet sky or stood for a moment on doorsteps for a breath of air. He had told them it was coming. He had shown them the path of honor and duty. He had told them what their past and their future both expected. Now, some bitterly, some gaily, they prepared to do it. Not all the news was bad that week.

Chapter II

*Death and sorrow will be the companions of
our journey; hardship our garment; constancy
and valor our only shield. We must be united, we
must be undaunted, we must be inflexible.*

—WINSTON CHURCHILL to the House of Commons

Time has dimmed and controversy obscured most of the
great battles of World War II. The literary arguments of
generals and admirals, the cold dissection of military historians, the tumultuous years between have combined to
blur our vision of what was once clear and urgent. The
Battle of Britain is an exception. Today, twenty years
after it was fought and won, it is fixed forever in the harsh,
hot sunlight of that terrible and glorious summer of 1940;
a great battle, a famous victory won at long odds and by
a narrow margin.

There must be many others who feel that twenty years
ago is as yesterday. In my mind's eye the pilots still sprawl
in the sun at Manston, the German bombers still move
aloofly up the Thames, I stand in a Kentish lane and see a
tormented Stuka trying to shake off a Hurricane. What we
have forgotten in the meantime is how much hung on the
issue. The future of the world was in the charge of a few

[13]

hundred high-spirited young men. Like the Battle of Waterloo it was very close thing.

The Second World War was fertile in decisive battles. El Alamein, Stalingrad and Normandy in the West, Guadalcanal, Midway and Kohima in the East. These are all battles that raise the question: what would have happened had they gone the other way? Future historians reviewing the war from a better perspective and, perhaps, unmoved by national considerations may agree on a single decisive battle. They cannot ignore the Battle of Britain.

The Battle of Britain was the first decisive defeat suffered by the German armed forces in the war. The defeat of the Luftwaffe saved Britain from invasion. The Germans had to win and hold air superiority over the sea they intended to cross and over the English beaches where they intended to land. To do this they had to destroy the Royal Air Force. They tried. They fought very well. But they were beaten.

So in the autumn the Luftwaffe turned to the bombing of London and other British cities, a task for which, incidentally, it was ill-equipped and poorly trained. The German army remained for some months poised on the French coast looking hungrily across the few miles of water that separated it from the fulfillment of victory in the West. Then late that winter many of its divisions began to move ponderously eastward.

By spring the armies were massing on the Polish plains ready for the leap upon Russia. Long columns of tanks and marching infantry wound through the Balkan passes.

The Afrika Korps appeared in the Western Desert. The roads the Germans took from the Channel coast after the Battle of Britain led to Stalingrad and Alamein.

In my boyhood old soldiers said there never would be another battle like Gettysburg. They meant that nothing they would ever see or do would equal those bloody hours on the hills and in the fields outside the sleepy Pennsylvania town. Today we can say with more accuracy that there never will be another battle like the Battle of Britain.

Air power in terms of the bomber and the fighter had a short, fierce life. Twenty years after the Battle of Britain that sort of air power is rapidly becoming as dated as the wooden walls of Nelson's navy.

Ballistic missiles with intercontinental ranges and destructive charges capable of wiping out a city are the new, perhaps the only, weapon of the ultimate war. Of course, we are told, the bomber and the fighter will have a role in war. Those who tell us are the airmen themselves; just as the admirals told us we could not do without battleships and the cavalry generals contended that cavalry had its role in modern war.

Air power, as the term is generally understood, first took shape in the closing years of the First World War. Its death knell sounded when the first German V-2 rocket exploded on London in the autumn of 1944. If there is another war, that sort of air power will have as little to do with the outcome as did cavalry in World War II. So the Battle of Britain not only was a decisive battle, fought primarily in the air, it also opened the brief era of great air battles fought by manned aircraft. ⌋

To understand that battle and its consequences, we have to return to Britain as it was in the summer of 1940 when the great trial of strength between the Luftwaffe and Fighter Command of the Royal Air Force began.

It was a strange world in which the certainties of twenty years had vanished, in which hope and resolution jostled despair and defeatism. What had occurred in the four months of April, May, June and July was so catastrophic that even the wisest could only slowly accustom themselves to the consequences.

The German army, navy and air force had won a series of victories unparalleled in the military history of Europe since the early triumphs of Napoleon. Although Adolf Hitler claimed most of the credit, the victories were the result of the brilliant planning of the general staffs of the three services, the efficient leadership provided by the German officer class, and the courage, training and ingenuity of the German soldier, airman and sailor.

In April the Germans challenged the British in their own element, the sea, and overran Norway and Denmark. The German navy was severely punished by the Royal Navy, so badly indeed that it never truly recovered. At the end of June, 1940, the effective German fleet was one heavy cruiser, two light cruisers and four destroyers. There was also the U-boat fleet. But this had only a secondary role in the great enterprise the Germans planned.

The campaign ended, just as the German offensive in

the West began, with Norway and Denmark occupied by a German army that had been almost immediately victorious everywhere save at Narvik in northern Norway.

On the night of May 9–10 the German army, supported by the Luftwaffe, attacked France and the neutral states of Belgium, the Netherlands and Luxembourg. By the first of June the British Expeditionary Force had been driven into a small area around Dunkirk. From there it was extricated, largely due to the ingenuity, skill and courage of the Royal Navy, but partly, too, because of its own discipline, stamina and fighting qualities. The BEF fled westward across the Channel to lick its wounds.

The Germans then turned their full fury upon the French army, whose invincibility had been one of the strongest of the prewar myths. A series of smashing blows tore the Third Republic and its army apart. By the third week in June France had fallen, France, the foremost military power of the anti-German coalition, France, the wayward mistress of Western civilization, France, the free, France, the fountain of liberty. From the North Cape to the Bay of Biscay, the coasts of Western Europe were in German hands, Paris, Brussels, The Hague, Oslo, Copenhagen echoed to the tramp of German field boots.

Only Britain and her Empire and Commonwealth remained in the field. The British were in a sorry state. The army had lost most of its best equipment at Dunkirk. Contrary to the general belief then and afterward, the BEF had been completely mechanized and its equipment was far more modern than that of the French army. The Royal

Navy had been cruelly battered in the Norwegian campaign and in the Dunkirk operation. A total of twenty-five
destroyers had been sunk or badly damaged while evacu-
ating troops. The German navy now possessed U-boat
bases along almost the entire Atlantic coast of Europe,
thus extending the British fleet's convoy commitments.
The Royal Air Force had fought well during the Battle of
France and during the Dunkirk operation but its fighting
was on a small scale. It was known to be inferior in numbers and, most people thought, inferior in quality to the
Luftwaffe.

This series of almost incredible disasters and the war
situation that was their result had a contradictory effect
upon Britain and the remainder of the uncommitted world.
The resolute buoyancy that slowly emerged in Britain in
the summer of 1940, a buoyancy that was in marked contrast to the gloom among her friends, puzzled almost every
non-Briton who observed it. In Washington, where the
islanders' friends were aghast at the fate that had overtaken France and the similar fate that they believed would
soon overtake the British, the reports from London of the
wryly humorous defiance with which the British faced
their fate seemed almost frivolous.

Indeed, while the German forces in northeastern France
and Belgium concentrated during those long summer days
for the descent on the United Kingdom, almost everyone
in authority in Washington had just about given up hope.
Friendship, even affection, wishful thinking born of the
sober realization of what America's position would be if

England fell, none of these could begin to balance the long roll of German victories. No one should blame the military men, the majority of them, it should be noted, ground generals, who reluctantly concluded Britain's hour had struck and advised against sending large shipments of arms across the Atlantic. They were, as they conceived it their duty to be, military realists and they could see no hope. Indeed, since the battle soon to be fought in the air had no precedent and since the revival of the combative spirit of the British, military and civilian, had no rational basis, the military men, on the strength of their information, were quite right.

This is a story primarily of the Battle of Britain and the men of Fighter Command who fought it. But it cannot be seen in perspective unless it is seen against the background of the people whose sons were the pilots of that command and who, in a tremendous burst of energy and enthusiasm, provided both physical and moral bases for the fight. There was nothing in Britain that summer so remarkable as the drastic change in the attitude of the British toward the war.

The long, cold winter of 1939–40, the Phony War, had been a period of boredom and uneasiness. There were no air raids worth mentioning. There was little action on land. Isolated incidents like the pursuit and suicide of the pocket battleship *Graf Spee* off the South American coast were poor fare for a people who, when war was declared on September 3, 1939, had made up their minds it was time to stop Hitler. The idea that the Germans could be

vanquished by the inexorable pressure of the naval blockade, the attractive but illusionary suggestion that the German army would butt its brains out on the Maginot Line,
the stories of Germany's alleged shortages in oil and steel
—none of these convinced the British that this war, unlike
all others, could be won without a great national effort.
The Chamberlain government was still in power but the
people, as opposed to the Tory politicians, had no great
faith in its ability to fight and win a war.

Indeed, in the light of what had happened in Britain in
the ten years preceding the outbreak of war it is remarkable that the people were ready to support any ministry
or even to continue to accept the system of parliamentary
government under which they lived. The governments of
J. Ramsay MacDonald, Stanley Baldwin and Neville
Chamberlain have frequently been described as the worst
in British history. From 1931 through 1934 there were well
over two million people out of work each year. Unemployment and poverty stalked the dark, mean streets of the
great cities.

Abroad the totalitarian empires of Hitler and Mussolini
grew ever stronger while at home the electorate was lulled
by the promises of politicians who said something would
be done and then either didn't do it or took half measures.
A humiliating series of diplomatic defeats ended at
Munich.

The conduct of the successive governments of those
days has been held up to scorn and derision by contemporary critics. It is doubtful, however, whether if someone

had sounded the trumpet—as Churchill sounded it in 1940 —the nation would have responded. The shadow of the terrible bloodletting of 1914–18 still lay across the British nation. World War I was commonly accepted by the young, and by many of its disillusioned veterans, as a ghastly mistake in which fools were led into battle by knaves and incompetents. This encouraged pacifism.

In 1933 the Oxford Union voted "that this House refuses to fight for King and Country." In 1935 over 11,000,000 people signed a Peace Ballot. This somewhat contradictory document favored both a reduction in armaments and forcible resistance to aggression. Its name, however, gave the impression abroad that the British were desirous of peace at any price, an impression that Mr. Chamberlain's diplomacy did nothing to correct.

The impression abroad, particularly in the United States, that Britain was divided by class warfare, weakened economically, and largely pacifist was understandable in the circumstances. Compared to the shiny, new power of Germany, even of Italy, Britain looked old, tired and feeble.

"This was one of those awful periods," Winston Churchill later wrote, "which recur in our history when the noble British nation seems to fall from its high estate, loses all trace of sense or purpose, and appears to cower from the menace of foreign peril, frothing pious platitudes while foemen forge their arms."

True, the economic situation did improve slightly between 1935 and 1939. The general effect of this improvement seemed to be a greater concentration on the material side of life. The middle class especially was anxious to turn its back on the lightning in the European sky and return to that comfortable, familiar world with its assured future that had been threatened by the great depression. In London the world of politicians and newspapers fermented over foreign policy. But until the middle of 1939 this touched only a few thousands in London and a few thousands more outside.

It is no wonder therefore that the world, friend and foe alike, was unprepared for what happened to the British people in 1940 and was unable to comprehend the forces moving to the surface in the winter of 1939–40.

The British people's instinctive feeling that the declaration of war the preceding September had loosed great and destructive forces upon the world deepened under the impact of the winter war between Russia and Finland. Hostilities against the Soviet Union, which many British conservatives considered a greater menace than Nazi Germany, nourished the forlorn hopes of this class that somehow the war would end and, in the words of one gallant but not particularly bright officer I met in Lille, "we will all be marching against the Russians in the spring." These feelings represented a small but fairly influential group that never was completely submerged politically until the coalition government under Mr. Churchill took power in May of 1940.

In that winter of discontent before the great national effort of 1940, other vultures tore at the morale of the

British people. The Communists had made great headway in the thirties, posing as the only party that was thoroughly and actively anti-fascist. The great rightabout-face of the Communist party in August, 1939, when the Soviet-German pact was signed, alienated many of the newer converts to communism in Britain. But the party's new line that this was "an imperialist war" still influenced some of the lighter-headed members of the left. The palpable absence of any real fighting in Europe, of course, gave credence to the party's line that neither Britain nor France really intended to fight Hitler and that the whole business was a sham.

Restlessness in a war no one understood, doubts on the left and the right about the course the government had taken, the delays in obtaining the right equipment, inevitable after years of halfhearted preparation, all these infected the people of Britain that winter. The worshipers of Churchill and the left wing have combined to paint a picture of confused and even frightened people, suffering grievously from absence of leadership.

This picture has always seemed slightly distorted to me. It overlooks the somber realism of the British, a trait almost undiscernible save in times of stress. The apprehensions expressed so often that long, dark winter—one of the coldest Western Europe had known in years—concentrated on the pursuit of the war. Having gone to great lengths to avoid war, as they almost always do, the British were now convinced that, since it had come, it had to be fought and won. Very few people believed that Chamberlain could win a war, very few accepted the versions presented by the right or the left of what the war was about.

Although they were at war they found to their surprise, and quite often to their disgust, that little had changed. The blackout made a difference at night. But in the cities the revelers could find plenty of restaurants and night clubs. In the country the customary round of sherry parties and country club dances continued with the excuse, familiar in the opening phases of all wars, that these would help morale. There were more men in uniform on the streets and sprightly young officers filled the better bars. But there were hundreds of thousands of other young men for whom there was no place in Chamberlain's war.

Rationing had been introduced but it was not severe. Theaters reopened in London. The newspapers faithfully reported the snippets of information about naval and air actions and occasional patrol encounters on the front of the French army. They strove to provide the illusion of war. But it was not enough, and deeply, sorrowfully the British knew it was not enough.

The German triumphs in Scandinavia and Northwest Europe ended the sense of frustration with so strange a war. But they did little to inform the people of what lay ahead. The enemy's victories did, however, dissipate the clouds of confusion about what the war meant. By the middle of June, even the dullest witted could recognize that it was now victory or defeat, survival or destruction.

But they did not—how could they?—envisage the form their trial was to take. Much has been made of the French illusion about the strength of the Maginot Line. The British had their own illusion. This was that great wars were conveniently fought well away from British soil. They had whipped Napoleon's marshals in Spain and the great master himself in Belgium. The Kaiser had been defeated in France. To the veterans of 1914–18, a very large group in the Britain of 1940, the absence of a front in France, by which they meant a trench system, was unthinkable. They clung to this illusion even after France fell. I can remember the startled disbelief in the face of an elderly major of gunners in a Plymouth pub the day I returned from Brest after the second evacuation.

"You mean to tell me," he said, "there was no line anywhere. How in God's name are we going to fight a war without a line?"

The train carried us to London through a golden summer afternoon. Arthur Pilkington and I lay on some mailbags and slept. Occasionally we peered through the windows at the fat and peaceful countryside. At Paddington there was the old familiar, cheerful clamor. Later I walked through the Temple from the office to the Savoy. Here were quiet, peace and dignity; stones speaking of laws greater than kings or commoners. Here was a mature strength. But how much strength?

Twenty-four hours earlier life had been lived to the accompaniment of the roll and crash of falling bombs and the thud of artillery. Lives, cities, countries were disintegrating.

Undoubtedly there had been parts of Louvain or Lisieux

as secure and quiet as these gentle courts. Now they lay broken and black. Surely I had seen elderly French couples as serene in their confidence of victory as those two over there. But now and for some weeks past life and war had been reduced to the simplicity of holding on long enough to get out. The civilians, those who fled and those who remained, wore that look of anxious strain seen on the faces of those caught in some great natural catastrophe whose immense dimensions they only dimly understood. The dead refugees lying grotesquely sprawled in the ditches into which they had been flushed by Luftwaffe machine-gun fire, the ancient French 75 at a road block held by a handful of elderly artillerymen, the frightened whores from Paris in Le Mans—these had been life since May 10.

Now this was London. There were sandbags around the entrances to buildings, to be sure. There was the blackout. The barrage balloons bobbed in the setting sun. But the restaurants and the pubs were full. Men said they were in the ministry of this or that and gave the impression it was terribly important. People talked of getting away for a few days in August. But on the east coast for many a night you could hear the guns across the Channel.

Yet the strain of greatness in adversity must have been very close to the false surface. From this unlikely beginning came the great renaissance of activity and resolution that enabled the British to endure the Battle of Britain, the long bombing of London by manned bomber, V-1 and V-2, and the harsh years of physical sacrifice and effort in

austerity that lay ahead until, nearly five years l[
war was won.

The first great national test lay ahead. In their [
to that challenge the British offered, not for the first time,
testimony of the help lasting values give to a free society
in adversity. But it is pertinent to note that the Battle of
Britain began with the British in their favorite military
posture: with their backs to the wall.

Chapter III

As England, in spite of the hopelessness of her military situation, has so far shown herself unwilling to come to any compromise, I have decided to begin to prepare for, and, if necessary, to carry out an invasion of England.

—ADOLF HITLER, War Directive No. 16

In war it is always an advantage to know exactly where you stand. This was an advantage, one of the few, held by the British. They knew they were in the last ditch, that they had to fight and win or go under. The Germans, on the other hand, having won a tremendous triumph, were uncertain of how best to exploit it into final victory. After the fall of France the Wehrmacht, which had moved with such savage precision in Poland, Scandinavia and Western Europe, was faced with a novel military problem. Hitler encountered a political situation no less novel.

In the British people and their new leader, Winston Churchill, the German Fuehrer found enemies who, although impressed, were not shaken by his victories and who were in no mood to listen to proposals for peace. This obstinacy baffled the Germans at the time. If wars were decided on the basis of pure logic, the British were licked.

To fight on would only invite further disaster. Seen against the background of recent events on the Continent, even the reasons the British gave themselves—when indeed they stopped to think about it—for fighting on seem wildly optimistic.

In the second half of May, when military opinion held that only a fraction of the BEF could be evacuated from Dunkirk, the Prime Minister asked the Chiefs of Staff to report on "British Strategy in a Certain Eventuality." The reply was:

"Our conclusion is that prima facie Germany has most of the cards; but the real test is whether the morale of our fighting personnel and civil population will counterbalance the numerical and material advantages which Germany enjoys. We believe it will."

Nothing about the air force. No mention of the navy. The United States does not appear to have figured in the conclusion. Only morale. No wonder Hitler failed to understand them.

Hitler has often been considered, and not alone by Germans, as a man of great vision, one who understood the ramifications of national and international power and could exploit them with rare success. But in the weeks following Dunkirk and the fall of France his vision failed him. We know now that he had cherished a rather ingenuous admiration for the British Empire and that he believed its dissolution would benefit only the Japanese, the Americans and the Russians.

As late as July 19, three days after he had issued the

famous War Directive No. 16, he made a speech in the Reichstag containing what he called "a final appeal to reason and common sense." In his view he had made "determined and honest efforts to achieve friendship with the British Empire—an empire which it was never my intention to destroy or even to harm."

Count Ciano, who was in Berlin at the time, confided to his diary that Hitler "would like an understanding with Great Britain." This love-hate relationship for Britain is, I believe, one of the keys to Hitler's behavior during that summer. The lack of decision at the apex of the Nazi war machine undoubtedly affected the generals of the army and the air force and the admirals. Hitler waited for some sign that the British were ready to call it quits; his approach to the problem of invasion, indeed the language he used in War Directive No. 16, is curiously uncertain.

This was hardly the type of encouragement required by the fighting services who were called upon to plan and carry out what to the Wehrmacht was a new, mysterious and potentially dangerous kind of operation. The three German fighting services commanded the efforts of some of the best military brains in the world. They were the repositories of wide experience in every type of military operation save one. The German forces had never carried out a large invasion across the sea against a prepared and resolute enemy. In this, and perhaps in this alone, they were behind the British, who since the eighteenth century had been combining the operations of the navy with those of the army. Over the years, from the night that Admiral

Saunders deposited Wolfe's army at the right spot at the right time for the attack on Quebec until the Narvik battle, the two services had been working together. In the process they had accumulated experience and a familiarity with the problems of amphibious warfare totally lacking in the German forces.

Only a nation with this sort of experience behind it would have dared to send a few score marines ashore on the French coast in July of that year. This raid, harbinger of bigger things to come, had no military significance. To the painstaking, precise Germans, such seemingly off-the-cuff operations were folly.

Much has been made of the disputes and conflicts within the German High Command during the preparations for invasion. It is certainly true that in this period the generals and the admirals failed to give the impression of august infallibility they had conveyed during previous campaigns. But we must remember that they were contemplating an operation of immense importance in conditions about which they knew only by hearsay. They were bothered by Hitler's "on again, off again" attitude and they suffered from the rivalries among his courtiers that beset the supposedly totalitarian Third Reich.

German planning for the invasion is an integral part of the story of the Battle of Britain because the plans finally adopted made the Luftwaffe the key to invasion. If it won, the invasion could proceed.

Although War Directive No. 16 was not issued until July 16, the invasion of England had been contemplated by one service, the German navy, since May. The navy's role in the victories in France, Belgium and Holland had been a minor one; possibly its planners were anxious for a less subsidiary role. The army, inflated with prestige, paid less attention, save for one or two farsighted officers like Guenther Blumentritt, who in retirement—how comforting are the pictures that can be conjured from the fire on a winter's night—realized that had the army moved and the plans been ready Britain might have been invaded immediately after Dunkirk.

May 21 was one of the best of the many good days experienced by the German army that spring. For it saw the Panzer divisions pushing through Abbeville to the Channel coast. The British, French and Belgians in the north were thus cut off from the main French armies in the south. Great operations lay ahead and Hitler may be pardoned for his lack of attention when Grand Admiral Erich Raeder, the commander in chief of the German navy, raised the idea of an invasion of England in an interview. Raeder's planners had been examining the problems of invasion since the previous November. They had concluded that an operation on large scale across the North Sea was a possible means of defeating the British. As is customary in all governments, the buck was passed from the navy to the army and then to the air force. The army didn't like the look of the thing. The air force wouldn't touch it. As far as we know, it was never forwarded to the rarefied atmosphere of the Oberkommando der Wehrmacht, the Supreme Command of the Armed Forces.

Hitler showed no interest in either the idea or the details of the plan explained to him by Raeder. In the circumstances he showed good sense. The French army had been savagely mauled but it was not defeated, the British were fighting stubbornly. This was the moment for fighting the battle of the day rather than contemplating the battle of the future. This was Hitler in his practical, military vein, and the unknowing British had cause to be thankful. Had the Germans begun preparations for invasion then, the outcome might have been different.

Raeder raised the issue again on June 20 when the military situation was vastly different. The British were back on their island. The French were defeated. The Italians were in the war; an event which at the time seemed of enormous significance. But once again the Fuehrer showed little interest in either the plans or the material requirements the navy put forward as the conditions for a successful invasion. But Raeder's tenacity was great.

At the time, however, he was encountering both the army's preoccupation with regrouping and re-equipment after the Battle of France and Hitler's delusion that the British would make peace. There were also senior officers and officials who contended that the navy and the air force would be able to strangle the seaborne trade of the British Isles and thus bring Churchill and his government to surrender without severe German losses.

Distasteful though the whole idea apparently was to the army, it was Field Marshal Wilhelm Keitel who on July 2 took the step that was to lead to the Battle of Britain and to defeat. On that day an OKW order, signed by Keitel, announced that "The Fuehrer and Supreme Commander" had decided that "a landing in England is possible, provided that air superiority can be attained and certain other necessary conditions fulfilled."

The wording reflects Hitler's divided state of mind. He does not order an invasion. He says it is "possible." And the order notes that preparation is to begin on the basis that the invasion is still a plan "and has not yet been decided upon."

"Provided that air superiority can be attained. . . ."

This was the key to the German preparations. The German navy had observed with interest, and possibly with a certain trepidation, the success of the Luftwaffe against the British warships during the Norwegian campaign. This lesson was very much in the minds of the German naval planners as they prepared for an invasion. Raeder raised his price.

On July 11 at a naval conference he told Hitler that no invasion fleet should put to sea until the RAF had been destroyed and the British navy driven from the Channel. This job was to be given to the Luftwaffe. Hitler agreed that invasion was only a last resort to force Britain to sue for peace, a curious description of an operation that, once begun, would have to be carried out to its obvious conclusion of occupation of Britain. Well before the essential directive, therefore, the burden of making the invasion possible had been placed upon the Luftwaffe.

Directive No. 16 said:

As England, in spite of the hopelessness of her military situation, has so far shown herself unwilling to come to any compromise, I have decided to begin preparations for and, if necessary, to carry out an invasion of England.

This operation is dictated by the necessity of eliminating Great Britain as a base from which the war against Germany can be fought. If necessary, the island will be occupied. . . .

I therefore issue the following orders:

1. The landing operation must be a surprise crossing on a broad front extending approximately from Ramsgate to a point west of the Isle of Wight. . . . The preparations . . . must be concluded by the middle of August.

2. The following preparations must be undertaken to make a landing in England possible:

(a) The English air force must be eliminated to such an extent that it will be incapable of putting up any substantial opposition to the invading troops.

(b) The sea routes must be cleared of mines.

(c) Both flanks, the Straits of Dover and the western approaches to the Channel . . . must be so heavily mined as to be completely inaccessible.

(d) Heavy coastal guns must dominate and protect the entire coastal front area.

This operation, whose code name was "Sea Lion," began, it is obvious, with certain initial disadvantages in concept. Only Hitler could have believed that after a preparatory program that included an offensive against the RAF, extensive mine-sweeping and mine-laying operations, and the registration by heavy artillery upon the coastal area it would be possible to mount a "surprise crossing."

Indications multiplied that Hitler's heart wasn't in it. As Peter Fleming points out, seven months had been allotted to planning for the invasion of France. Yet this operation of a type the Wehrmacht had never yet attempted was given only four weeks. Did he really believe the operation would be necessary? Three days before the directive was issued he was still puzzled by the unwillingness of the British to make peace.

Nonetheless the orders went out. The divisions lying along the French coast were set to field training which seemed childish to veterans who had humbled the French army. The navy continued the movement of submarines and light coastal craft to the western ports. But the most urgent preparations concerned the air force.

Superficially the Luftwaffe was the most spectacular and successful of the German armed services in the early summer of 1940. It was the unknown element in the German victories. The tight V's of Stukas preceding the armored columns, the waves of heavy bombers and clouds of fighters were horribly familiar to the broken forces of the enemies of the Reich and to millions of noncombatants who watched them in newsreels.

Compared to the army and navy it was a young service. Like the RAF, it had attracted daring spirits who found the tradition and peacetime routine of the older fighting armies oppressive. Again like the RAF, the Luftwaffe had established a tradition of daring and gallantry during the first war. Von Richthofen was still a resplendent name in Germany. And had not Reichsmarschall Hermann Goering

himself been a redoubtable fighter pilot? T
of the Luftwaffe carried themselves with th
air common to services not yet fully teste
driven the Polish air force from the skies (n
trick, but the civilians didn't know that), the
tions along the Meuse had broken under the impact of the
Stukas (although Guderian and his panzers had something
to do with that too), and the British and French had been
harried to the sea by the fighters and bombers (of course
they got away at Dunkirk, but that could be blamed on
the weather).

As an air force the Luftwaffe suffered from one obvious
deficiency. In prize-fight terms, it had never had to get up
off the floor after a knockdown. Three great campaigns
had been won. But the air force had not yet encountered
in strength an air force that was not afraid of it. Its career
had progressed from triumph to triumph without a severe
or even a temporary check. True, some of the pilots who
had fought over Belgium and northern France had returned with minatory accounts of the quality of the British
fighter aircraft and their pilots. But in the heady rejoicing
after such a complete victory their stories were discounted
or overlooked. Here was the Luftwaffe on the lip of
Europe, the all-conquering Luftwaffe, and over there, just
a few minutes away, lay England, a close-packed, industrial country, an easy target.

Yet the task before the Luftwaffe was one for which it
had not been thoroughly trained and which was foreign
to the concept of air power as practiced by Germany. The

ـuftwaffe was an independent service. But its strategic and tactical independence was severely circumscribed by the massive, traditional authority of the army chiefs. German military greatness had been built upon the army. The influence of its leaders was paramount. They regarded the Luftwaffe as an important adjunct to the ground forces. They did not see it as an independently decisive service. To them it was "flying artillery," whose primary role was to blast a hole in enemy positions when these delayed the advance of the tanks and infantry. The Ju 87, the famous Stuka, had been highly successful in this role during the Continental campaigns largely because it had not been opposed by strong air forces. It was to prove almost useless in the Battle of Britain.

Many Luftwaffe officers had studied strategic bombing operations and accepted such operations, carried out at long range, as the ultimate expression of aerial warfare. This was not, however, an integral part of national military doctrine as it was proclaimed by the Supreme Command. Strategic air war, that is, the bombing of an enemy's industrial and communications installations, was secondary in the eyes of the German military leaders to tactical operations by the air force in support of the ground forces. In Britain the air force commanders after long and violent argument with the elder services had won the acceptance of strategic air warfare as an essential part of the RAF's mission. As we shall see, emphasis upon the strategic versus the tactical role of the air force left Britain perilously short of fighter aircraft in 1940. But long before the outbreak of war the RAF had planned the four-engined bomber that was to carry the air war deep into Germany.

In the Wehrmacht no such independence of mind or authority existed in the air command. Its leaders were dominated by the ground generals; in fact in many cases they were themselves army officers with little or no experience in air operations.

The Luftwaffe was venturing into the unknown. Hitler had committed it to a type of battle for which there were no precedents. The primary task was familiar—destroy the enemy air force. But this was to be done against an air force fully alert to Germany's intentions. Fighter Command would not be sitting on its airfields with planes nicely aligned so that a single pass by three German fighters could knock out a squadron. The targets this time would not be shaken infantry inadequately protected by antiaircraft guns but dockyards, cities and ports protected on the ground by many guns and in the air by many fighters. The British would be flying planes as good as or better in some respects than the German fighters. Finally the battle had to be fought at what in those days was a considerable distance from the German bases over an unknown country whose freakish weather was a byword among fliers.

Yet the young men lazing through the pleasant days along the rim of Europe were confident. They were unbeaten. They were the strongest air force the world had ever known. And, very important, they were living in a golden period of German history when everything appeared to go just right for the Third Reich. To them defeat was not remote, it was unthinkable.

"I went to dine with my cousin in the air force," a German captain of infantry told me after the war. "It was early September and there were many new faces in the squadron. I could not believe it. Transfers, I thought. Perhaps, leave. But no, when I departed Sigismund told me. They were having much difficulty with the English. Many losses. But they would win in the end."

On August 10, when the battle was under way, the Luftwaffe had an over-all strength of 4,295 aircraft of which 3,242 were combat planes ready for action. Of these 2,355 were deployed for service against the United Kingdom in Luftflotten (air fleets) II, III and V. Serviceable aircraft in this force on August 10, 1940, were: 998 long-range bombers, 316 dive bombers, 702 single-engined fighters, 261 twin-engined fighters and fighter-bombers, and 78 long-range reconnaissance aircraft.

The main burden of the fighting in the battle was carried by the two famous Messerschmitt planes, the single-engined 109 and the twin-engined 110. The bombers were the Heinkel 111, the Dornier 17 and the Junkers 88. The Junkers 87, the dive bomber, played a subsidiary role.

By supersonic standards the performance of these aircraft was pathetic. The Junkers 88 was the fastest bomber. It could do 287 miles an hour at 14,000 feet. It could carry more than two tons of bombs on a trip to London and return while the Dornier could carry just over a ton and the Heinkel, which jogged along at 240 miles an hour at

14,000 feet, about the same. The Ju 87, the feared Stuka, had a range of only 360 miles with a bomb load of 1,100 pounds and a speed of 245 miles an hour at 15,000 feet.

But by the standards of 1940 these were formidable bombers. The ruins of Guernica, Warsaw and Rotterdam testified to their effectiveness. They were commanded at the operational level by experienced officers confident of their weapons and their personnel. They had reason to be. The Luftwaffe pilots and air crews in 1940 were of an exceptionally high standard, courageous and experienced. Their weakness, discerned early in the battle by British pilots, was that any disruption of their battle plans by enemy action resulted in complete disarray.

The three Luftflotten assigned to the battle were Luftflotte II, commanded by General Albrecht Kesselring and based in northeast France, Belgium and Holland, Luftflotte III, under General Hugo Sperrle in north and northwest France, and Luftflotte V, under General H. J. Stumpf in Norway and Denmark. Kesselring had commanded Luftflotte I in Poland. Sperrle had led the Kondor Legion in Spain in 1936 and 1937, where his successful attacks on virtually undefended Spanish cities like Guernica had given the strategic warfare advocates in the German Luftwaffe command an inflated idea of what their forces would be able to do against the British.

These massive forces, of course, could not be employed at once. Before an offensive of this magnitude could begin stocks of fuel and bombs had to be moved from Germany to the new airfields. In many cases the fields themselves had to be improved, the necessary ground installations, including antiaircraft emplacements, built and repair and maintenance units established. Some of the squadrons needed rest and refit. Others, whose experience was confined to close support of ground forces, had to be trained for a new type of operation. "We found out then," a Luftwaffe captain remarked after the war, "that we had forgotten about navigation in the Stuka squadrons."

So the Luftwaffe took a month to prepare for its great effort; a month, which, we will see, was a godsend to the British.

The Germans' lethargy is incredible. The Luftwaffe, admittedly, had much to do in the way of reorganization and refit. But it had been given the task, in a directive of July 16, of not only destroying the RAF but preventing all attacks on the German invasion forces, destroying coastal defenses in the landing areas, and smashing the reserve formations of the British army behind these areas. With this sort of directive, how could any delay have been countenanced? But the preparations moved slowly.

Hitler's own attitude toward the operation hardened gradually. On July 21 he told his commanders that he had decided that invasion was the "most effective means of bringing about a rapid conclusion of the war." This announcement was made five days *after* he had issued Directive No. 16. Again the Fuehrer stressed the necessity of obtaining "complete mastery of the air." The German services themselves were confident that this could be attained. Colonel General Franz Halder was told that between two and four weeks would be needed to smash the RAF. Halder, by nature austere and cautious, apparently believed it. With this sort of optimism endemic at the higher levels of command and with Hitler something less than wildly enthusiastic, it is not surprising that the Luftwaffe took its time. In any event it was not until the beginning of August, two full months after the last British ships had sailed westward from Dunkirk, that Hitler gave the order for the start of the air offensive. The invasion itself was tentatively scheduled for the third week in September.

Nothing is so revelatory of the German air force's confidence as the leisurely manner in which Goering moved. It was not until August 6—people in England that week noticed that the days were drawing in—that the Reichsmarschall addressed his senior commanders at Karinhall, his sumptuous house and headquarters, on the task before them. There is no record of Goering's speech. What we know of it has been pieced together from the recollections of Sperrle and Kesselring.

The elimination of the RAF was laid down by Goering as a primary task of the three Luftflotten. This was to be done in two phases. First, there was to be a sustained offensive against the fighter airfields in England south of a line between Chelmsford and Gloucester. The airfields were to be made unusable for the British fighters and the installations destroyed. The RAF was to be attacked in the air wherever it was found. The whole thing, Goering said, would take four days. One is reminded of Napoleon on the morning of Waterloo telling his marshals that the battle would be over by lunch. The second phase, Goering admitted, might take four weeks. This was to be a methodical attack on other RAF bases to the north of the line Chelmsford-Gloucester.

After this attack had been concluded, Goering informed his air generals, there would be no RAF left to fight. He also ordered that while these two consecutive assaults were mounted against the British bases there should be day and night attacks on the British aircraft industry.

The offensive would begin, Goering said, on August 10 and the first day's attack would be given the code name "Adler Tag" (Eagle Day).

The Reichsmarschall's confidence had reached the point where he half hinted to friends that invasion might not be necessary once the Luftwaffe had completed its job. Here again we get a glimpse of the peculiar endurance of the idea that, for reasons never quite clear then and obscure now, invasion never would be necessary. It is not, after all, surprising to find it in Hitler, whose military pronouncements sometimes were indistinguishable from those of an opium smoker. But it is strange to see traces of the same attitude in Goering, who beneath the fantastic costumes and the ribald, gusty manner concealed a sharp and realistic mind.

Knowing what we do of the comparative strengths of the two forces, the Germans' confidence that day at Karinhall is almost incredible. But, as we know, the Luftwaffe had never been beaten; it had never even been seriously challenged.

Goering's program included some interesting points of reference for the remainder of the battle. For instance, aside from the bombing attacks on the aircraft industry's scattered factories, the Luftwaffe did not contemplate heavy bombing of civilian areas. That came later and it came because the German bombers and fighters had been unable to do the job assigned—destroy the RAF.

But things were different then for the Luftwaffe. As July slipped into August the construction work on the new bases in France, Belgium, Holland, Denmark and Norway was completed. The gasoline, machine-gun and cannon ammunition, and bombs arrived from Germany and were stored. Replacements in pilots and aircraft reached the units.

The heat lay heavy on the land that summer and the haze sometimes obscured vision. But the young men of the Luftwaffe high over the Pas de Calais in the summer dawn could glance across the Channel to where England lay, ripely green. To them it must have seemed so easy in those last days before the whirlwind caught them up and they plunged into one of the great battles of history.

Chapter IV

To fight England is like fighting fate.

—Lord Dunsany

The progress of the Royal Air Force toward the point where it was fit to fight the Luftwaffe was studiedly unspectacular. It was a long process often delayed, occasionally helped by politicians. Men of genius played their part but much of the credit belongs to those airmen, scientists and civil servants who labored anonymously in the dreary years while an uncaring Britain drifted toward war. It was, in fact, a very British operation.

Two decisions stand out. The first was taken in 1934 by an intense, rather austere professional airman named Hugh Dowding who was then member of the Air Council for research and development. Dowding increased the armament of the two new fast, single-wing monoplanes being developed by the Supermarine and Hawker firms from four to eight machine guns. The aircraft were the Spitfire and the Hurricane and they were Dowding's principal weapons when in 1940 he directed Fighter Command against the Luftwaffe.

The second decision came after a lengthy, thorough scientific experiment that began toward the end of 1934.

H. E. Wimperis, then the director of Scientific Research at the Air Ministry, suggested that a scientific group be assembled to study means of locating hostile bombers attacking Britain. The Air Ministry was already alive to the threat implicit in the new German bomber production although, with the exception of the member from Epping, no one in politics appeared unduly apprehensive.

Mr. Churchill made a minatory statement to the House of Commons on February 7 of that year.

Britain unless it took proper precautions might find itself, he said, "confronted on some occasion with a visit from an ambassador and may have to give an answer, and if that answer is not satisfactory, within the next few hours the crash of bombs exploding in London and the cataracts of masonry and fire and smoke will warn us of any inadequacy which has been permitted in our aerial defenses. We are vulnerable as we have never been before."

The "cursed, hellish invention and development of war from the air has revolutionized our position," Mr. Churchill emphasized. "We are not the same kind of country we used to be when we were an island only twenty years ago." His words, like so many others in the next five years, went unheeded. In the clubs people thought "Winston was becoming a bit of a crank about this air business." In the House of Commons the government found him irritating.

The initiative taken by Wimperis, however, had led to important progress. A committee was established with H. T. Tizard, chairman of the Aeronautical Research Committee, as chairman. The other members were Professor A. V. Hill, Professor P. M. S. Blackett and Wimperis. They deserve well of their country.

Unlike most committees organized by a government, this one moved with exemplary speed. At its first meeting it decided that the detection of approaching aircraft by radio should be explored and that the committee should ask help from R. A. Watson Watt, then superintendent of the Radio Department of the National Physical Laboratory.

By February 12, 1935, Watson Watt had sent a memorandum to the committee that led to revolution in air warfare and contributed massively to victory in the Battle of Britain. Watson Watt had been experimenting on calculations of the height of the ionosphere by the reflection from it of radio waves. He explained that waves could be similarly reflected from the metal parts of an aircraft and that this reflection could be recorded.

The committee was enthusiastic. It agreed to ask the Treasury for £10,000 for experiments and approached Air Marshal Sir Hugh Dowding for support. Dowding recognized the importance of Watson Watt's claim. But he knew to his cost, as most professional airmen, soldiers and sailors did in those days, how difficult it was to get any sum out of the Treasury. And in the piping times of peace £10,000, then approximately $50,000, was important money to the watchdogs at the Treasury. So Dowding suggested a demonstration.

Two weeks after the report had gone in, a Heyford

from the Royal Aircraft Establishment at Farnborough spent a monotonous day flying between Daventry and Wolverhampton. At Weedon, over which the pilot passed three times, his progress was being "watched." The pilot was flying on a course corresponding to the lateral center of the Daventry 50-meter radio beam. At Weedon, Watson Watt and his associates were grouped around a wireless receiver to which a cathode-ray oscillograph had been attached.

Peering into the oscillograph the scientists saw the radiation from Daventry as a straight line. But when the Heyford entered the path of the beam they saw the line oscillate until when the aircraft was overhead they were able to observe a deviation of over an inch. In the words of the Royal Air Force's historians, "without specially designed equipment, without control of wave length, and without any great transmission power, it had been demonstrated beyond doubt that electromagnetic energy was reflected from an aircraft, and that these reflections could be depicted visually by the cathode-ray apparatus."

The committee was impressed. Dowding was told that "we now have, in embryo, a new and potent means of detecting the approach of hostile aircraft, one which will be independent of mist, cloud, fog or nightfall, and at the same time be vastly more accurate than present methods."

That was on March 4, 1935. A few weeks later Foreign Secretary Sir John Simon and Lord Privy Seal Anthony Eden were told by Hitler in Berlin that the Luftwaffe had already reached parity with the Royal Air Force. Perhaps

But it is hard to escape the conclusion that the ...rall of the Luftwaffe in its decisive test came appreciably nearer as a result of those experiments in the shack at Weedon in February, 1935.

For those who cling to the attractively romantic notion that the Battle of Britain was won by brilliant improvisation the speed and certainty with which the British moved toward the establishment of a detection device is a corrective. Watson Watt and some of his staff were made available to the Air Ministry's research by the Radio Research Board. By the end of March sites had been chosen for laboratories and towers and design of suitable transmitting and receiving apparatus had begun.

The new device was known as "radio direction finding" or r.d.f. The popular term "radar" (radio direction and ranging) did not come into British use until 1943 when it was adopted as part of the effort to establish a joint nomenclature for the American and British services.

By the autumn of 1935 the Air Council, that is, the general staff of the Air Ministry, was encouraged by the results of experiments to recommend the construction of a chain of ground stations from Southampton on the south to the river Tyne in the northeast. The Treasury, always cautious, agreed to the building of five stations. The principal chain of twenty stations was not authorized until the summer of 1937.

When war came there were twenty radar stations in Britain. These could detect planes flying at medium height at a range of one hundred miles and a special device called i.f.f. (identification friend or foe) had been developed to distinguish enemy from friend. Finally the radar stations had been incorporated into the air defense system.

The advantage given the British by the possession of radar is incalculable. Without radar the air defense of Britain would have required thousands of fighters, so many in fact that there would have been little money or resources left for the other services. With radar Fighter Command squadrons, although fewer in number than the Germans, could be concentrated at the points of maximum danger. And throughout the battle the British knew when the Germans were coming and approximately where. There were many early difficulties and shortcomings in its operation, but radar played an important part in the winning of the battle and the war. By September, 1940, radar cover for the British Isles was established in a chain of stations formed like a reversed "L." The top of the "L" was the Shetland Islands in the north. The angle was the bulge of Kent and the horizontal arm followed westward to Land's End in Cornwall. From these stations the beams reached out roughly one hundred miles to "see" aircraft over the sea or rising from airfields in Holland, Belgium and France.

Other inventions helped. Fighter Command's efficiency was increased by Pip Squeak, a device that enabled pilots to report their position to a control station on the ground and a high-frequency radio telephone that made possible clear, direct speech between the controller on the ground and the pilot.

In the preceding chapter we noted the German delay in mounting the air offensive against Britain. This delay was particularly advantageous to the British in the radar field. For after Dunkirk urgent priority was given to the construction of more radar stations and other installations of the air defense system. In those long, hot weeks of June and July, while the Luftwaffe made "assurance double sure" the RAF's scientific defenses were growing stronger. Oddly enough, although the Germans were aware of the existence of the British radar system at least a year before the outbreak of war, not much value was attached to this system of detection at high levels. The Germans had experimented with radar in 1938 and 1939 but with little success. Goering, as director of the Four-Year Plan, refused to allot funds for radar research to the Luftwaffe commanded by Goering.

German scientists took the line that if they had been unsuccessful it was not to be expected that the plodding British would get anywhere. Both Goerings, the air marshal and the director of the economic plan, believed them. This was a grievous error.

Radar would only attain maximum effectiveness, of course, if the British fighters, when they reached their enemies, were capable of defeating them. The development of British fighter aircraft is a less instructive story than that of the development of radar largely because the story included a basic conflict over the strategy and tactics of air war.

The problem of the air defense of Great Britain had

worried the Royal Air Force almost since the end of World War I. Its senior officers naturally were quick to realize that the development of the long-range bomber ended isolation. Churchill, it will be recalled, was still trying to get this lesson through the politicians' skulls sixteen years later. But without radar the air force planners faced an almost impossible task in defending Britain. The country, they reasoned, could wind up with a defense budget that concentrated on the production of fighters and left little money for anything else. The cost of fighter defense seemed in the early 1920's to be prohibitive. Consequently, the Air Staff concluded that air defense must be offensive, that it should take the form of massive bombing attacks upon the enemy's air industry and air force over his own territory. Once that was done the air force could turn to the secondary, and by then infinitely easier, job of destroying the enemy's industrial system. With this offensive theory firmly established in the minds of its most distinguished air officers, the RAF continued to establish two new bomber squadrons for every new fighter squadron until 1938.

For much of the period between 1918 and 1938 the RAF, like the army and the Royal Navy, suffered from a lack of new equipment. It was the general British view in 1934 that Britain's service aircraft were outclassed in speed and load capacity by the new metal monoplanes then coming into service on American commercial airlines.

But in July, 1934, the government finally bestirred itself. What was then called the Home Defence Air Force was to

:eased from 42 squadrons to 75. Of these 47 would
mber and 28 fighter squadrons. The satisfaction
aroused by this Cabinet decision among politicians evapo-
rated, however, the following March when Simon and
Eden got the news from Hitler that the Germans had already reached air parity with Britain and intended to continue building until their air force was equal in strength
to the combined British and French air forces. Again the
British Cabinet raised the ante. This time the strength of
the Home Defence Air Force was raised to 121 squadrons,
or 1,512 aircraft. But the emphasis was still on bombers.
The Cabinet was given the impression that the heavy,
four-engined bombers would win a war. What the RAF
later called "the big bird boys" dominated service thinking.

The RAF had a long way to go in fighter construction.
Its best fighter in 1934 was the Fury II armed with two
machine guns and capable of 223 miles per hour at 15,000
feet. But 1934 was a vintage year for British planning. For
that year it was decided to equip the new fast monoplanes
being developed by Supermarine and Hawker with eight
rather than four machine guns. This gave a single Spitfire,
made by Supermarine, or Hurricane, produced by Hawker,
about as many machine guns as a British brigade at the
front in 1914. The superior firepower of these two machines was one of the principal reasons why they attained
and held the upper hand over the Luftwaffe in the Battle
of Britain.

Before these two new machines could reach the squadrons and play their role in the defense of Britain, the ground installations of the RAF had to be expanded enormously. New airfields, new schools, new camps, new bombing and gunnery ranges were built.

Britain is a small, cramped island. Such expansion provoked the wrath of landowners, farmers, industrialists. This wrath ran unchecked by any lead from Downing Street, where Mr. Chamberlain was still certain of his ability to arrange peace with the German Chancellor. It was also exacerbated by the obvious fact that the new installations, especially the ranges, would raise Cain with wildlife. The British have never become accustomed to the fact that they are an industrial nation, preferring to regard themselves as green-thumbed farmers who for the moment happen to be turning out electronic equipment or marine engines. The idea that precious wild fowl might be disturbed provoked bitter denunciations of the RAF and hundreds of fanatic letters to the newspapers. The Germans, who tend to regard the British as an invincibly frivolous race, must have thought their national assessment correct when the laborious efforts of the RAF to build an adequate defense were bedeviled by the bird lovers. Fortunately for Britain's future, no horses were endangered by the expansion.

With the bird lovers at length placated, the fields could be built. The number of RAF airfields rose from 52 in 1934 to 138 soon after the outbreak of war. In addition many civilian airfields were taken over. By modern standards, of course, most of these fields were rather rough and ready.

Few had concrete runways. On most the only hard surface was in front of the hangars. But operational equipment for control and the living quarters were a considerable improvement. They had to be, for they were soon to receive a flood of civilian airmen accustomed to better conditions than the peacetime RAF and far from hesitant about demanding decent living accommodation.

When the war began Fighter Command was like a mettlesome colt, half trained and wholly untested. Leadership in the first year of the war was exerted largely through squadron leaders and wing commanders. What Fighter Command needed more than tactical leaders was a man who understood the task before it and was not to be diverted from obtaining the necessary weapons, someone of real strategic imagination, technical insight and unswerving purpose. This man was found in the person of Air Chief Marshal Hugh Dowding.

Dowding's character was a sharp contrast to the grotesque buffoonery of Goering. He commanded young men whose hilarious high spirits became a byword yet he remained rather unapproachable; his nickname "Stuffy" suited him. He had led a fighter wing in France in 1916 and he realized far better than many of his friends or his critics just what his young men were facing. This knowledge put an edge to his tongue during his long, difficult, but eventually successful battle to get the planes he needed.

Need them he did. At the time of the Munich crisis in September, 1938, Fighter Command had only 406 aircraft in its home defense squadrons. None of these were Spit-fires and there were only five squadrons of Hurricanes. This was about 60 per cent of the strength that Dowding regarded as providing reasonable security for Britain. This grave weakness in modern fighters was certainly a factor in the political decisions taken that autumn although not, of course, the decisive factor.

A word about the command system of the RAF at the outset of the war.

General strategic policy and the allotment of resources was the province of the Cabinet of which the Secretary of State for Air was a member. The Air Council executed this policy in its sphere with the chief of the Air Staff responsible for over-all control of operational policy. Under him were the officers commanding the separate commands such as Fighter Command, Bomber Command and Coastal Command. These men employed the forces available to them to obtain objectives sought by the chief of the Air Staff in response to higher instructions. Below them were the group and squadron commanders fighting the war on the tactical level; their army counterparts commanded American regiments or British brigades or battalions.

The year of grace bought at Munich, disgrace was the view of some, was a boon to the RAF. While the civilian population might have been lulled temporarily by the promise of "peace in our time," the fighting services, especially the RAF, were not. Production of Hurricanes and Spitfires rose in late 1938 and early 1939 and by the

[57]

outbreak of war reserve of about two hundred of these valuable aircraft had been assembled.

The outbreak of war found Fighter Command still numerically inferior to the Luftwaffe fighter forces. The British had only 608 first-line fighters and another 320 in reserve. But the percentage of Spitfires and Hurricanes in the command was rising rapidly; qualitatively it was a much stronger force.

When the Battle of Britain began the British position, due largely to the losses suffered in May and June and to the relatively slow rate of fighter production and replacement, was not much better. From May 10, when the Germans attacked, until June 18, when the last flight of Hurricanes left France, the RAF lost 477 fighters, 219 of them from Fighter Command, and 284 pilots. By the middle of July, when what the British consider to be the preliminary phase of the battle opened, Dowding, by stretching his resources to the limit, might have been able to put 600 day fighters into the air. Reckoning the normal tactical strength of a fighter squadron at twelve planes, this was fifty squadrons. The program called for 1,450 pilots. In fact there were 1,253 available. Some of these were needed for the six squadrons of Blenheims and two squadrons of Defiants that formed part of Fighter Command but did not play significant roles in the battle. Others were untrained or half trained.

Four operational groups guarded the British skies, No. 11 Group, commanded by Air Vice-Marshal K. R. Park, defended southeast England with headquarters at

Uxbridge. This group, guarding both the great citadel of London and the most probable area of invasion, bore the heat of the battle. When the fighting was most intense, September 7, 1940, the group could call on twenty-three squadrons, fourteen of Hurricanes, seven of Spitfires and two of Blenheims. In this and in all the other groups the squadrons were allocated to sectors. In No. 11 Group these were Tangmere, Kenley, Biggin Hill, Hornchurch, North-olt, North Weald and Debden. As we shall see, the sector stations, controlling from two to four squadrons, were immensely important to the conduct of the battle on the British side.

The second most important group was No. 12, defending the eastern counties and the Midlands. It was commanded by Air Vice-Marshal T. L. Leigh-Mallory with headquarters at Watnall near Nottingham. At the crisis of the battle, what Mr. Churchill liked to describe as "the crunch," No. 12 Group had fifteen squadrons, six of Spitfires, six of Hurricanes, two of Blenheims and one of Defiants.

Farther north was No. 13 Group, whose parish was northern England, Scotland and Northern Ireland. Its headquarters were at Newcastle-on-Tyne and it was commanded by Air Vice-Marshal R. E. Saul. He had under command on September 7 three squadrons of Spitfires, eight of Hurricanes, one of Blenheims and one of Defiants.

No. 10 Group defended southwest England under the command of Air Vice-Marshal Sir Quintin Brand with headquarters at Bath. This was the smallest of the groups.

At the height of the battle it had only ten squadrons. But four of these were of Spitfires, four of Hurricanes, one of Blenheims and one of Gladiators, the last of the old biplane fighters.

Fighter Command in those memorable days was predominantly professional still. But the Auxiliary Air Force squadrons played an important role. No. 11 Group had six such squadrons, County of London, City of Glasgow, County of Gloucester, City of Edinburgh, City of London and County of Nottingham. Like Britain's territorial army in the piping times of peace the AAF was composed of part-time warriors. When the test came they were as good as the best.

Finally the command included at the height of the battle a squadron of the Royal Canadian Air Force, two Polish squadrons and a Czechoslovakian squadron.

The RAF's principal weapon was the Hurricane. This fighter had a maximum speed of 316 miles an hour at 17,500 feet and a service ceiling of 33,200 feet. In the Mark II the speed was boosted to 342 miles an hour at 22,000 feet and the service ceiling raised to about 36,000 feet. The Spitfire's performances were better. But in 1940 "the Spits" were outnumbered by the Hurricanes. At any rate the Spitfire Mark I did 355 miles an hour at 19,000 feet and had a service ceiling of 34,000 feet. The British fighters were armed with eight machine guns, whereas the Messerschmitt 109 had two machine guns and two millimeter cannons and the Messerschmitt 110 had six machine guns and two cannons.

The legend has grown up that the Spitfire won the Battle of Britain. It was a graceful aircraft with an arresting name. Because of its superior speed the Germans respected it more than the Hurricane; the worried call "Achtung, achtung Schpitfeuer" from Luftwaffe pilots helped build the legend. But it was the Hurricane, marvelously adaptable and very hard to hurt, that played the major role in Fighter Command's battle.

Aircraft, detection systems, command—all these were important. But the Battle of Britain could not have been won without the pilots. In her extremity the old kingdom drew upon a great national resource, her young men. They did not fail, and it was their courage and daring that used the tools and won the battle.

They came from every county and from every class. As the youngest of the services, the RAF had fewer "families" than the army or the navy. Throughout these services at the outbreak of war were officers whose military ancestry could be traced back to an officer in the same regiment at Waterloo or to a captain of one of Nelson's ships. In that sense, and perhaps in that alone, the RAF was much less professional. The young regular officers had grown up with flying. The senior officers could remember the harum-scarum days of single combat above the western front in the First War.

From Munich onward the regular officers were augmented by Volunteer Reserve pilots who had completed their flying training. These were the "weekend pilots," the "long-haired amateurs" who came from university squadrons or had flown with their local flying clubs on week-ends. In time of course these amateurs were to outnumber the professionals. But in 1939 and 1940 they were new. The professionals looked at them askance. Senior officers wondered, unnecessarily, what they would be like when the time came.

The fighter pilots, professional and amateur, were as blithe and valorous a group as any in the war. Many actively disliked the military part of their training. They said with wonderful gusts of profanity that they could not understand why they had to learn to form threes on barrack square or study military etiquette. Others were willing enough, but hated the technical side of flying; they couldn't be bothered to learn about engines or map reading. But one and all loved flying itself.

The Volunteer Reserve added a certain worldliness to the small, closed world of the professionals. Here were gay young men from Oxford and Cambridge ready to spend a month's pay on one wild "night out" in London. Here were intellectuals, equally gay, who would sit up half the night discussing the war and its origins; subjects which the professionals left to the politicians and the high command. Here were solemn Scots and fervent Welshmen from towns and villages with queer Celtic names and some scores of brawny young men from Canada and Australia and South Africa and New Zealand who had joined the air force in Britain.

They drank and they wenched. Their behavior on leave was a scandal to senior regular officers of all three services

and their own immediate commanders found them a handful. As the battle wore on, they developed an esprit de
corps which few services have ever approached. Like all
services with a high morale, they had a tendency to look
down on men less happily situated. Their name for the
British Expeditionary Force, after Norway and Dunkirk,
was "Back Every Fortnight" and they held naval officers
to be humorless fellows to be teased with questions about
"the sharp end" and "the blunt end" of their "boats." The
fame they won impressed them very little. I recall that
shortly after the Battle of Britain some solemn fellow in-
quired in the *New Statesman and Nation* whether these
pilots might in the future form the cadre for a British
Fascist party. When I read this to a group of pilots it was
greeted with roars of incredulous laughter.

The grass is long on their graves now; those whose
graves are known. I wonder sometimes what they would
think of the great memorial that rises on the hill by Runny-
mede that bears the names of those whose bodies were not
recovered. Probably, "memorials are moldy, old boy, much
better have a noggin before closing time." If heavenly
justice has done its job, I hope there is some celestial pub
where they can stand, with the top button of the tunics
unbuttoned, pewter mug in hand, and talk about the
"popsie" they met at the Savoy and "that ass of an adjutant who thinks this is a bloody Guards regiment."

Chapter V

. . . the Battle of Britain is about to begin. Upon this battle depends the survival of Christian civilization. . . . The whole fury and might of the enemy must very soon be turned against us. Hitler knows that he will have to break us in this island or lose the war.

—WINSTON CHURCHILL to the House of Commons

The Battle of Britain was shaped to an extraordinary degree by a number of decisions taken by the British before the fighting actually commenced. Of course, once battle was joined, the tactical decisions taken on both sides influenced the course of the fighting from day to day. But it can be argued that there would not have been any battle, certainly not one that would be remembered for twenty years, were it not for the decisions made beforehand. Two of these decisions have been mentioned earlier: the order to proceed with the development of a means of locating approaching aircraft that ultimately produced radar and Dowding's conclusion that the Spitfire and Hurricane must have an armament of eight machine guns. Now we come to the decision that was probably the most difficult of them all. This was the British government's refusal to send more fighter squadrons to France.

This decision has been the source of French accusations of British betrayal in an hour of need. It has been portrayed as an individual decision taken by Winston Churchill. Certainly Churchill, as prime minister, had the unhappy duty of saying no to the French government. But the refusal was based on the best professional advice; in other words, on the advice of Dowding who, in those tumultuous days, seems to have seen the future more clearly than many of his military and political superiors.

When the German storm burst upon the Allied forces in France and Belgium four squadrons of Hurricanes were dispatched to France. On the fourth day of the battle, thirty-two Hurricanes and pilots, two full squadrons, were flown out. There were six squadrons in France when the Germans attacked on May 10, so that by the 14th the British fighter strength had been doubled.

But on that day the full extent of the first German successes became known in Paris and London. The German Fourth Army had broken through in the neighborhood of Dinant, tearing great holes in the French defenses with their Stukas and panzers. The British bombers and fighters had fought continuously. By the night of May 14 the RAF had only 206 aircraft remaining out of the original strength of 474.

While General Heinz Guderian drove his armor westward and the Stukas sought new targets, Premier Paul Reynaud of France made the first appeal for help to London. "The hard question of how much we could send from Britain without leaving ourselves defenseless and thus losing the power to continue the war pressed itself hence-forward upon us," Churchill recalled in *Their Finest Hour*. Reynaud said he wanted "ten more squadrons" if "we are to win this battle, which might be decisive for the whole war" and he wanted them "today."

The first British reaction was to move four more squad-rons of fighters to France. But on May 16 Churchill lis-tened in Paris to the vehement pleading of Reynaud and General Gamelin, the Allied Commander in Chief. He de-cided to ask the Cabinet for the transfer of another six squadrons. This the Prime Minister knew would reduce Fighter Command's strength to twenty-five squadrons, which he thought he had been told was the minimum number compatible with safety. Dowding, who now ar-rived in London with fire in his eye, denied later that he had ever called twenty-five squadrons the absolute mini-mum. This, he explained later, was an Air Staff figure based on the assumption, now invalid, that the Germans would not possess bases for the Luftwaffe in the Low Countries and northern France.

Fighter Command's chief outlined the position as he saw it to Air Chief Marshal Sir Cyril Newall, chief of the Air Staff, on May 16 while Churchill, in Paris, was learning the full extent of the French disaster.

"If an adequate fighter force is kept in this country," Dowding wrote, "if the Fleet remains in being and if the Home Forces are suitably organized to meet invasion, we should be able to carry on the war singlehanded for some time, if not indefinitely. But if the Home Defence Air

Force is drained away in desperate attempts to remedy the situation in France, defeat in France will involve the final, complete and irremediable defeat of this country."

When the War Cabinet met that night Dowding put his case to the politicians. This was simply that if the air battle in France continued to devour fighters at the present rate the supply of Hurricanes would soon be exhausted. Newall supported him, declaring that a few more fighter squadrons "whose loss might vitally weaken the fighter line at home" would not make the difference between defeat and victory in France.

These arguments were decisive. On May 19 Churchill halted by order the transfer of further fighter squadrons to France. Fighter Command had enough, just enough, fighters to play an important, and sadly underestimated, role in the evacuation from Dunkirk. It retained a nucleus of modern fighters and trained pilots for the great trials to come in the Battle of Britain. If we accept that battle as one of the turning points of the war, the first step on the road to Germany's defeat, the decision in the long run was of the utmost importance to the Allied cause.

In the agony of defeat the French were not ready to forgive. At the time many Britons, too, felt that more was due to an ally than had been forthcoming from the British government. Both the French politicians and generals and their friends in Britain, however, underestimated the military chaos, the despondency and the defeatism that pervaded the French forces from about May 21 onward. Nor could they understand the speed and precision with which the Germans were advancing. I was in France and Belgium until the Dunkirk evacuation and later in France again before the final surrender. The country was literally disintegrating, militarily, politically and morally. Had the British sent the squadrons the French demanded, after a day or two they would have been swallowed in the terrible convulsion shaking France. Fighter squadrons need more than the planes and pilots; they need fuel, ammunition, repair facilities and airfields. How long would these have been available?

A sadness pervaded those fatal weeks. The British decision exacerbated French feelings. But in the end it proved the right decision. For the RAF was able to fight and win —by a very narrow margin—the first decisive battle of the war.

After Dunkirk and the fall of France, the RAF, indeed all the armed services, plunged into weeks of hectic activity. The army was clamoring for the equipment lost in the battles on the Continent and in the evacuation from Dunkirk. The Royal Navy dockyards and many civilian dockyards were patching up the destroyer force which had been roughly handled during the evacuation. The RAF, certain from its top commanders down to the rawest pilot that it would fight the next battle, was the busiest of all.

By the middle of July six new stations, known as Chain Home stations, had been added to the radar system and six other Chain Home Low-Flying stations installed. Balloons were added to the barrages that nodded over most ports and cities and their number grew to 1,466. The Observer Corps and the searchlight batteries were reinforced. There remained, however, a desperate shortage of anti-aircraft guns.

When France fell there were only 1,204 heavy and 581 light AA guns in Britain although the table of organization called for 2,232 and 1,860 of each type. In the next five weeks 124 heavy and 182 light guns were added but a considerable proportion of these were needed for training. The opening of the battle found Britain still alarmingly short of these weapons.

Fighter Command benefited from the furious activity of Lord Beaverbrook, the Minister of Aircraft Production. Four fighters were added to each of thirty Hurricane and six Spitfire squadrons. These were to be flown, in an emergency, by pilots who otherwise would have been resting or on leave. The navy contributed 68 pilots to the command. A new fighter group, No. 10, was formed to protect the western ports within easy reach of enemy bombers striking from newly occupied airports in France. In the factories, in the repair hangars men worked until they literally fell asleep on the job.

It was a golden summer. The sun that shone across the Channel on the busy airfields, the battalions solemnly training for landings on a hostile shore, shone too on a London that pursued its daily life with a touch of defiance. Soldiers played civilians at cricket on village green and the *Times* advertised "A Good Selection for your Summer Holidays in Scotland." Women were urged to "Spend Wisely at Harrods." Freya Stark's *A Winter in Arabia* pleased the literary critics and that now-forgotten figure, King Carol of Rumania, was the subject of an authorized biography.

Although they stood in peril, the incurable English were not to be bullied by that peril into accepting any wartime regulations that they thought affronted the things they were fighting for. H. G. Wells complained bitterly to that national forum, the letter column of the *Times,* about the plight of refugees from nazism who had been interned by the government and Gilbert Murray wrote magisterially to the same column "I tremble for any democracy which yields either to party faction or to mob hysteria." The nation might be prepared for total war, but it was to be a total war in which the English would abide by their own rules.

The theaters and cinemas were full. *Gone With the Wind* was thrilling audiences with its somewhat fanciful record of another war. Stanley Holloway and Cyril Ritchard were in *Up and Doing* and Vic Oliver appeared in *Black Velvet.* As is their custom in times of trial, the English spent a good deal of time laughing at the war and their own efforts. Many people, including senior officers of the three services, thought this lighthearted approach a poor preparation for what was to come. The English laughed harder.

Flora Robson opened in *We Are Not Alone.* But they were and no one seemed to mind. The depression that had set in with the fall of France lifted. There was excitement in the air. At Westminster the incomparable voice of the Prime Minister reminded his countrymen of both their peril and their opportunity. The setting sun fell over airfields on which the number of fighters grew steadily, on shaky lines of Home Guards, on divisions perilously short of weapons standing to near the invasion coast. So the English waited.

Unlike the fighting in France, the Battle of Britain did not open with a sudden, massive attack. All through June the Luftwaffe had launched small, widely scattered attacks, mostly by night, against British targets. Most daylight attacks had been confined to the ports. Gradually in the early days of July the attacks extended inland. They were heavier in scale, more bombers, more fighters. The sirens sounded in Wales and on the east coast. Then the Luftwaffe revisted the ports Dover, Weymouth, Portland, Plymouth and again the attacks were heavier. The convoys moving through the Channel were heavily attacked.

In those days you could lie on the cliffs near Dover and watch the British ships come steadily onward from the north. Against the blue sky there would appear, suddenly, the tight formations of German bombers. Then the dive by the Stuka—the Luftwaffe had not yet recognized its unsuitability for this battle—the high scream, the thud of the explosion, the towering column of water white through the middle and glinting with sunshine at its top, and then, the column subsiding into the Channel, the rusty old collier plowing placidly onward. Then another bomber and another attack and in your ear the high keen of British fighters. Very small, they shone against the sun. Then, faintly, the chatter of machine-gun fire. Perhaps a puff of smoke from a plane to be followed by a flicker of flame and a long plume of black smoke as the aircraft plunged. It was hard to believe that in that minute of machines in the sky men fought and that in that burning plane one was fighting for his life. There was always a feeling of relief when a parachute blossomed white against the sky. As swiftly as it began the fight would be over. In the Channel the convoy steamed ahead. The antiaircraft fire dwindled. It was quiet now on the cliffs and the breeze brought all the scents of summer.

The attacks were not yet on a large scale. There were seldom more than twenty German bombers and the same number of fighters involved in a single foray. But Fighter Command, still recovering from the exertions of the past two months, was hard pressed. July 8 saw about three hundred sorties flown. The attacks on Channel shipping forced Dowding to move some of his squadrons to forward airfields where they were in better position to intercept the Germans. Even then in 1940 shipping, coastal as well as oceanic, mattered terribly to the British. What later developed into the Battle of the Atlantic, the longest battle of the war, began in late 1939 and 1940 around the coasts of the British Isles.

One of the oddities about the Battle of Britain, perhaps inseparable from air warfare, is the difference of opinion over when it actually began. Basil Collier, whose chapters on the battle are a magnificent day-to-day account, puts the start at July 10. The Germans generally consider Adler Tag, Eagle Day, as the opening round. But, although there was a heavy German attack on August 8, the Germans regard Adler Tag as August 13 although there is not much difference between the scale of their attack that day and the one on the preceding day. My view is that the earlier date, July 10, is the more satisfactory one. By then it was clear that the Germans would have to destroy Fighter Command if they wished to invade Britain and from that day onward, with mounting strength, they sought to do just that.

The fighting on that day in some ways foreshadowed all that was to come later. Radar, for instance, played an important role. The stations in southeast England reported a large number of German aircraft gathering beyond Calais and the British fighters were in the air in time to intercept. Throughout the battle the Germans usually outnumbered the British. That was true on July 10. In fact in one sharp encounter three Hurricanes took on twenty Messerschmitt 109's escorting some Stukas. The early battles inevitably disclosed some inadequacies both in the radar stations and in the use of the reports they provided. The first estimates of the strength of the German attack often erred so that five or six British fighters would find themselves dealing with forty or fifty German aircraft.

The efficiency of the radar stations varied. In the west of England the stations, possibly as a result of inexperience, occasionally were surprised by an enemy raid. In Kent, the stronghold of No. 11 Group, the fighters sometimes got as much as twenty minutes' warning. Time was essential. It took a Hurricane about fifteen minutes to climb to 20,000 feet, a Spitfire about three minutes less. The majority of successful attacks by the British were launched from above the German formations. But before the fighters got to their chosen altitude, the radar message had to be received, the probable course of the German force calculated and plotted, and the orders transmitted to the defending formation.

Throughout the battle a heavy and terrible responsibility rested upon the officers who controlled the movements of the defending forces. They had at their disposal just so many aircraft and these could remain in the air for only a certain length of time. Radar reports a German formation moving toward the Channel. Is it a large formation intent on a real attack? Is it a feint? How many fighters can be sent to deal with it? If Squadrons X, Y and Z are sent, what will be left if a second major attack is launched at another point? To a great extent victory or defeat rested on the judgment of the controllers at the groups. And their decisions could not be reached after long and careful weighing of the evidence. They could not wait for further reports. They had to act and act quickly. And on what they did depended the lives of men in the air, the safety of a city, even the security of the realm itself. Because they knew how perilously small Fighter Command was, they were, at the outset, reluctant to commit large forces to battle. For they realized that the Germans with their numerically superior forces could afford to squander formations in mock sorties designed to wear down the endurance of the British pilots and consume precious gas.

Some of the problems of those early days disappeared as the battle progressed. The radar operators, for instance, became proficient in estimating the strength of enemy formations as their experience grew. But they still suffered from an inability to give a reliable estimate of the height of the attacking forces. The difficulty, of course, was that the Germans invariably climbed to gain height as they crossed the Channel. Squadron and flight leaders of the RAF soon learned that, unless otherwise ordered, their safest course was to gain the maximum height as soon as they left the ground. Such tactics, of course, involved the risk of missing the German formation. But height, which gave the attacker the advantage of a dive out of the sun on an unsuspecting enemy, was of such paramount importance that the risk was one that had to be taken.

The fighting on July 10 and 11 cost the Germans twenty-eight aircraft while the British lost ten planes. Henceforward such figures will be important in this narrative and readers with a good memory will find them very different from the figures given out at the time by both sides. For instance, on August 15 the RAF claimed it had destroyed 182 German aircraft and had probably destroyed another fifty-three. The German archives show that the Luftwaffe lost seventy-six planes that day. How did these exaggerations originate?

One explanation lies in the character of air combat. Pilots flying at speeds of five miles a minute seldom can reach a balanced, accurate judgment on the amount of damage they have done. They press the button, the machine guns fire, they see a puff of smoke from the enemy aircraft's engine, and it passes out of sight. They claim a "kill" or a "probable." But before the intelligence officer can ask further questions the squadron is off again. As Max Aitken points out, two or three pilots might attack and damage the same German aircraft at various times during a fight and each pilot might reasonably and honestly claim he had destroyed the enemy plane. Again, British pilots were ordered not to follow damaged enemy planes when they fell out of the battle; presumably many of these limped homeward. The fault lies not with the pilots but with the authorities who allowed claims, which by the nature of things could only be estimates, to be given to the public as facts.

Whatever the accuracy of the claims, no one can doubt their tonic effect upon the British people.

To them, alone, overworked, often sleepless, the figures were exhilarating. Here was something tangible, something they could understand. Here was their country fighting for its life in a new element and winning the fight. A comment by John Martin, principal private secretary to the Prime Minister, exemplifies the lift these figures gave even to so stouthearted a combatant as Churchill.

On the night of September 15 Martin gave his master the news from all over the world. Shipping losses were rising. Plans and stratagems had gone awry. But as Martin finished his account he said, "All is redeemed by the air.

We have shot down one hundred and eighty-three for a loss of under forty."

It is time now to turn from the beleaguered British to their formidable enemies across the Channel. During the opening phase of the battle, from July 10 to the end of the first week in August, the German Air Staff was guilty of a number of mistakes in their assessment of the British defense. These mistakes were paid for by the crews of the Luftwaffe's bombers and by its fighter pilots. The elementary mistake was the German command's failure to understand that the improvements in radar and radio equipment gave Fighter Command far more flexibility than would have been possible a year earlier. This can be traced back to German science's deep-rooted doubts about the practicality of radar and the scientists' somewhat arrogant conclusion that, since they had not been able to progress very far, the British would be similarly unsuccessful.

Knowing that the defending fighters got their orders from the ground, the German Air Staff concluded that the squadrons were tightly controlled by their bases and could not operate away from a given area. This conclusion was a mistake. The British inferiority in numbers forced flexibility in defense upon the RAF.

"You cannot be strong everywhere" is a well-known maxim of land warfare. But the increased efficiency of radar and the ground control staff enabled the British to give the Germans the impression that Fighter Command could anticipate their tactics and intercept their formations with forces which, although numerically inferior, slowly attained a qualitative superiority. In retrospect it is clear that in the opening phase of the battle the Germans were prone to rely almost entirely on their overwhelming quantitative superiority. While the great offensive that was to begin on Eagle Day was thoroughly prepared, little thought was given to tactics in the preliminary period.

Not that the Germans were idle. The planning for Operation "Sea Lion" occupied the admirals and the generals. They soon found themselves at odds. The army, which had been dubious about the project from the outset, soon concluded that invasion to be successful must be on a front from Dover to Portland which was broader than the navy desired, that there must be a secondary and diversionary landing north of Dover, and that the whole operation called for the use of 260,000 men in two waves, the first of 100,000 picked troops. The German navy, although accustomed to taking second place to the army, could not stomach such grandiose plans. With considerable sharpness the admirals pointed out that they had transports and warships to support and protect only one landing and that the project of bringing in 160,000 men and all their equipment on the second wave of invasion would require approximately 2,000,000 tons of shipping. The army argued that if the invasion was concentrated, as the navy wished, on a single front the first wave would be badly mauled by the defending British who would be able to concentrate their forces in one area. The navy retorted that if the initial attack was made on a number of fronts, as the army suggested, the invasion force would suffer heavy losses from attacks by the Royal Navy and Bomber Command of the RAF. Each of the protagonists in this argument meanwhile harbored serious doubts about the ability of the Luftwaffe to carry out the essential preliminary to invasion—the elimination of the RAF.

The interservice rivalries, the swings from overoptimism to black pessimism, and the confusion and uncertainty of the Germans in this period can be regarded as amusing only by the callow. A useful corrective is the thought that the Americans and British, each with a long tradition of amphibious operations, needed two years, from 1942 to 1944, to plan the invasion of Normandy. Even with the great resources available to them the Allied staffs frequently altered their plans during those years and the final tactical plan did not take shape until early in 1944. The Germans, asked to prepare an operation that was outside their military experience, can be pardoned for failing to produce a foolproof scheme in eight weeks.

The weakness lay not in the planning but in the lack of conviction. As early as July the navy talked about postponing the invasion until 1941 unless the U-boats and bombers brought Britain to her knees. The army, with less understanding of the problem of overseas landings and support, made up in confidence what it lacked in experience. The final plan called for the use of thirteen divisions with twelve in reserve and with eleven divisions landing in the first wave. The command was given to Field Marshal Gerd von Rundstedt. Given the necessary transport by the navy and support by the Luftwaffe, the army was sure the job could be done.

Hitler, as we have seen, persisted in thinking that the British might surrender without a fight. On July 19 he made a peace offer.

"In this hour," he told the Reichstag, "I feel it to be my duty before my own conscience to appeal once more to reason and common sense in Great Britain as much as elsewhere. I consider myself in a position to make this appeal, since I am not a vanquished foe begging favors, but the victor, speaking in the name of reason. I can see no reason why this war need go on. I am grieved to think of the sacrifices it must claim."

The speech caused some merriment in Britain because of its revelation that Hitler had a conscience. It had very little effect otherwise. Hitler's offers of peace had encountered the law of diminishing returns long before the war began. The British press, in fact, rejected the peace offer before the government had time to reply. Then Lord Halifax, the Foreign Secretary, rejected what the Cabinet and people alike had interpreted as an offer to surrender.

This British reaction was received by something very like consternation in Berlin. Count Ciano sensed "ill-concealed disappointment" among the Germans and noted that Hitler "would like an understanding with Great Britain" since he knew that war with the British would be "hard and bloody." Hitler himself, it is apparent, still envisaged a cheap victory, even after the British rejection of his offer. On July 20 he stressed to the attentive Ciano that "Germany's strategic position, as well as her sphere of influence and of economic control, are such as to have already greatly weakened the possibilities of resistance by Great Britain, which will collapse under the first blows."

I was in a pub off the road from Dover to London on the evening of the 20th. The consensus of the patrons was that Hitler must be dotty. Who the hell, they asked rhetorically, would trust him? But they wasted little time on the Germans and the fighting. Their sensitive palates had detected, they said, a decline in the quality of the beer and they were much more indignant about this than over the German bombs on Dover.

This was a period when the English habit of considering war as a series of small, personal affronts tried the nerves of foreigners in their midst. Tea rationing had begun on July 9 and a good part of the conversation was devoted to what "my old woman" had said about the government as a result. There were also some highly disrespectful remarks about the appointment of the Duke of Windsor to be governor of the Bahamas. Of the prospects for survival and victory, nothing.

Throughout those weeks in which the Luftwaffe prepared for its great onslaught the unnatural calm continued. There was a good deal of well-bred tut-tutting because the Eton and Harrow cricket match had been confined to a single day; Eton defeated her ancient rival by a single wicket.

In the *Times* of July 11, the day after the opening of

the battle by British reckoning, there was room for a two-paragraph story on the acquisition by a London firm of existing stocks of wallpaper designed by William Morris. The personal column included the notice: "Mr. and Mrs. H. A. Lermitte and Miss Lermitte having reached England would like to hear of any of their friends from France." What light relief there was came from the German propagandists, who at one juncture issued a report that the people of London were revolting against plutocratic cricketers.

On Bastille Day, July 14, the tall, aloof figure of General de Gaulle appeared in a ceremony at the Cenotaph in London. The days were sunny and Londoners, finding it difficult to travel, turned, as they have always done, to the Thames and their parks for relaxation. The late afternoons found them along the river's banks or sprawled coatless on the grass.

Gradually, almost imperceptibly the battle moved into the forefront of men's minds. On the morning of the 15th the public was gratified, but not especially surprised, to be told that eighty-five Germans had been shot down in the week ending on the 14th. The ringing of church bells had been forbidden except in case of invasion and an absent-minded rector was imprisoned for a week for galvanizing his parish with an injudicious peal. During that time there appeared, too, the first reports of American popular support for Britain. A Rupert Peyton of Shreveport wrote to the *Times* that Britain was "our first line of defense." The publication of extracts from his and similar letters may have done more harm than good. On the whole, the British were unprepared for and never thoroughly understood the great American debate over intervention in the war.

But in Washington the precise and steady mind of General George Marshall, the chief of the General Staff, moved, although for other more complex reasons, to a conclusion similar to Mr. Peyton's. The greatest American soldier of his day had already approved the shipment of rifles, machine guns and field guns to Britain. Now Churchill was asking for thirty or forty old destroyers, adding, with perfect truth, that "the next six months are vital." While Wendell Willkie emerged to become the Republican nominee and Franklin D. Roosevelt moved toward his third term, the War and Navy Departments kept their eyes on Britain. The generals and admirals did not need to be told of the perilous position of the United States should Britain collapse.

Roosevelt, perhaps moved by the pessimistic reports sent him by Ambassador Joseph P. Kennedy, was worried over two contingencies that seemed remote to the British government and people. Would Britain, he wondered, surrender its fleet or sink it voluntarily? The British hardly gave such things a thought. They were waiting and, although every day meant a further strengthening of the island's defenses, they found it tedious. If "they" were coming, let them come. On July 17 the *Times* published a quotation from Sir Francis Bacon that seemed particularly apt:

"Walled towns, stored arsenals and armouries, goodly races of horses, chariots of war, elephants, ordnance, artillery and the like; all this is but a sheep in a lion's skin, except the breed and disposition of the people be stout and warlike."

Chapter VI

*On the 8th of August, 1940, the RAF Fighter
Command took off to save everything, and between then and the end of September they saved
it all.*

—General of the Air Force H. H. ARNOLD

So August came. The eyes of Britain and, slowly, those
of the world turned to the air above the Channel, the
Downs, and the neat fields of Kent, Sussex and Essex. The
game, the young men of Fighter Command said, was "on
the table" but no tremor of anxiety was evident. Max Aitken, soon to win fame as one of the crack fighter pilots,
recalls that psychologically No. 11 Group was ready. The
pilots in those days said little about the war although they
would talk freely about their planes and their performance. No one made fine speeches about defending the
homeland; indeed they listened to Churchill's rolling oratory with indifference. Such things, their manner said,
were for the civilians. They had a job to do.

"Don't you believe all this bloody nonsense about the
Jerries turning tail and running," a pilot said on a misty
morning at Hornchurch. "They're bloody good, the Jerries.
They give me all the fighting *I* want."

[85]

Then he said casually something that must have been in many young minds:

"Course it makes a difference to us, fighting over England. You come in and you see it lying there, nice and green, gives you a good feeling, you know. Liable to start daydreaming unless you're careful. Bad thing, that. Wake up with a Jerry on your tail."

The Operations Section of the Luftwaffe on August 2 issued its first instructions for the conduct of the great offensive. There had been some dispute on the tactics to be used. Some German commanders wanted the number of bombers kept to a minimum; others sought a balanced attacking force of bombers and fighters. Adolf Galland, then a Luftwaffe major, and other German pilots remember a period when high authority thought the Spitfires and Hurricanes could be lured to battle by German fighters alone.

Good visibility naturally was important to the Germans if they were to open the ball with a smashing attack. Consequently, Eagle Day was twice postponed to August 13. Before it came, however, the Germans attacked heavily on August 8, 11 and 12. The raids on the 12th are especially noteworthy because they revealed that curious inconsistency in target selection that intermittently during the battle reduced the effectiveness of the offensive and helped the English.

Airfields at Hawkinge, Lympne and Manston and radar stations in Isle of Wight, Sussex and Kent were attacked. In retrospect it is clear that the German air force, knowing that its objective was the elimination of Fighter Command, should have continued these attacks. True, the damage done on the 12th was not crippling. Craters on the strips were filled in and buildings repaired so that three fields were ready for use in a few hours. Of the six radar stations attacked only one was knocked out, although all were damaged. All told the Germans made at least five major attacks that day and the bombers were well covered by fighters. The Luftwaffe lost thirty-one planes, Fighter Command twenty-two; not an impossible ratio to accept from the Germans' standpoint.

When Eagle Day and subsequent "big" days arrived, however, the Luftwaffe failed to return to the airfields and the radar stations on which the defense of Britain rested. One reason obviously was overconfidence. The Luftwaffe, on the basis of its pilots' claims, thought it was winning. Another reason was the Luftwaffe High Command's tendency to underrate the importance of radar. Finally the pilots themselves often failed to give a clear picture of the amount of damage they had done. When they did report heavy damage to an airfield, their stories subsequently were questioned by authority. For other German formations flying over the same area found themselves attacked by British fighters. The Germans, underestimating the flexibility of the British defense, concluded that the damage to the airfields had been exaggerated.

What sort of men fought that battle on the British side? Turn now to 85 Squadron. The pilots had returned from France with only three aircraft left and July found them flying from Debden and Martlesham north and northeast of London. The squadron had been part of the air component of the British Expeditionary Force and when I first met it in France during that long, cold winter of 1939–40, its young men were enjoying the phony war.

The public imagination has enshrined a picture of laughing, joyous young men, knights of the air. They could laugh and they were joyful, all right, when they had put their war to bed. But on duty they had a certain cold competence. They were what a later generation would call "pros" and, like all true professionals, they took their job with immense inner seriousness. This was always with them.

One night in May of 1940 in Lille the German bombers interrupted a mild celebration some of them were holding in a hotel. They felt good. The battle had been on for some days and, although everyone knew that things were going badly on the ground, the fighter pilots were confident. I stood at the window with Dickie Lee and watched the searchlights vainly probing the sky and listened to the people on the streets running for shelter.

"Those aircraft of ours are bloody good, old boy," he said. "Bloody good. Give us enough of them and enough trained pilots and we can hold them. But the brown jobs" —the army—"are having a poor show. Well, let's have some more of this champagne."

They got enough of the aircraft and they held them. Years later, reading Richard Aldington's *The Duke* I was reminded of a similar prophecy made by Wellington to

Creevey, shortly before Waterloo and, in distance, not so far from where we were standing that night. Give me enough of that article, said the Duke pointing to a British infantryman in the park at Brussels, and we'll pull the thing off. So they did. And so did the RAF. But Dickie was not there to see it. How he would have grinned when people talked about knights of the air or sang songs about a pair of silver wings. No, they were not knights but simple, brave young men who knew hardship and fear, ambition and defeat. There were enough of them, just enough, and they hung on throughout that summer and into September when the tide turned and their legend began.

On May 23 that was a long time in the future. That day the squadron got a new commander. His name was Peter Townsend, a grave, courteous man who seemed older than his years. A great deal, much of it untrue, has since been written about Peter Townsend. Let it be remembered that in those days when the survival of his country, perhaps the survival of Western civilization, rested on the courage, stamina and skill of a few hundred British boys, Squadron Leader Townsend was as good as the best. No one could have been better than that. He was shot down twice. In return, among twelve other successes, he got three German planes on August 18. When he left the squadron in June, 1941, he was on crutches.

For the squadron the first days of August were devoted to patrols over the convoys moving toward the Channel. "Another day of convoy patrols and no E/A (enemy aircraft) to liven things up," says the log for August 3.

By August 11 things were somewhat livelier. The taut language of the log is typical of the time.

Martlesham 11/8/40*—11:30. As usual patrols on convoys started with the dawn. At 11:30 hours while yellow section was on patrol with S/L Townsend D.F.C. as Yellow I. he sighted an E/A which he identified as a Do[rnier] 17 about 2 miles E of the convoy and at about 4,000 ft. At 1150 hrs he was within 300 yds of the Do 17 and slightly below, and gave it 2 three second bursts from under the tail; there was no return fire from air gunner, and E/A disappeared into cloud. When it reappeared S/L Townsend got in another 2 three second bursts, which put the starboard engine out of action and E/A went into a steep dive and disappeared into thick cloud. S/L Townsend could not follow as there were 20 plus Me [sserschmitt] 110 Jaguars in his immediate vicinity, and, at this moment, he heard the German leaders over the R/T interspersed with "September in the Rain" in broken English. He also saw a large splash which he thought to be a crashed aircraft, but was unable to verify as he had to engage one of the 20 Me 110's noted above, and slightly separated from his companions; he saw his bullets enter the starboard mainplane but observed no results. After several attempts to isolate another Me 110 and being attacked himself and having very little petrol and less ammunition he returned to forward base to refuel. At 1200 hours Pilot Sgts. Allgood and Hampshire were engaged by 7 Me 110's at 5,000 ft; the former dived on 1 Me 110 well below him and gave him a three second burst and E/A dived into the sea sinking almost immediately; the latter attacked another Me 110 below him and gave him one long continuous burst, and E/A went into a steep dive; he followed it down firing till all his ammunition was used; he observed bits falling off the E/A before breaking off.

* British style: day, month, year.

August 13, Eagle Day of the German war calendar, fell that year on a Friday. The hallowed weekend of peace was fast disappearing under the stress of war but people still regarded Friday as the end of the workweek and Friday night as a time for relaxation. Theatergoers were flocking to see Robert Donat in *The Devil's Disciple* and that night pretty girls and young men in uniform would dance at the Café de Paris, the Savoy and the Mayfair. Despite the barrage balloons, the sandbags and the blackout the war had not yet drastically changed British life, although it changed very fast in the next four or five weeks. Indeed, although it might have been Eagle Day for the Germans, the incorrigible British were discussing other birds. The *Times* had informed its readers with well-bred imperturbability that twenty-seven of them had written to report the continued call of the cuckoo in their districts and that all who had written agreed "that the cuckoo has this year been in finer form than usual."

The war was pressing in, however. Income tax had been raised. The taxes on wines, beer and tobacco rose. The Ministry of Food informed the population that cabbages, beans, cauliflowers, lettuces, turnips and tomatoes were "fine foods for health and vigor." Mr. Molotov reaffirmed Soviet neutrality to the world, saying that efforts to detach the Soviet Union from the German pact had failed. Sir Stafford Cripps had been talking to Stalin in the Kremlin without apparently much effect. The new book on Allenby had received generous reviews although its author was perhaps too busy to read them. He was General Sir Archibald Wavell and his reading that summer centered upon the intelligence reports on the Italian build-up in Cyrenaica.

The Germans started early. At 5:30 A.M. the radar picked up, at the then astonishingly good range of 110 miles, two German formations assembling over Amiens. Forty-five minutes later No. 11 Group had the better part of four squadrons in the air. It was soon evident they would not be enough. Radar reported another Luftwaffe concentration near Cherbourg and a fourth over Dieppe. By 7:00 A.M. the defending force had been just about doubled, although accounts differ as to the actual number of aircraft in the air. Ultimately about 120 British fighters were airborne from the Thames estuary around to Exeter. Even so, the British had to fight about two and a half times as many German planes.

Over eighty of these, bombers, came in over the Thames estuary. By some failure on the German side they were un-escorted and one formation was jumped by a squadron of Spitfires. With great courage the Germans pushed on to their targets while the gunners in the bombers engaged the Spitfires. A few of the bombers got through and did some damage to the Coastal Command station at East-church. The other German formation, hotly engaged by Hurricanes, was driven off after doing little damage.

Fighters escorted other bombers heading for the Royal Aircraft Establishment at Farnborough. This formation was engaged almost as soon as it crossed the coast. Again it failed to strike home. A formation of Ju 87's, heavily escorted, withdrew after making contact with British fighters.

There followed a strange episode in the battle. A force of Me 110's, minus the bombers it was supposed to escort, attacked Portland. The Me 110 lacked the maneuverability of the British fighters and in the short, sharp fight between the German force and squadrons from Nos. 10 and 11 Groups the invaders lost five aircraft very quickly. The German planning and operational direction on Eagle Day was not what one would expect on so important an occasion. Bombers had been sent in without fighter protection and fighters, with no bombers to protect, had ventured far afield and been brought to action by superior aircraft.

The Germans were not finished, however. The afternoon brought three other heavy attacks including raids on eleven airfields. On the left flank of No. 11 Group the Germans hammered targets in Kent and in the Thames estuary. But heavy cloud impeded the bombers and, although one formation got through to bomb Detling, others were so hotly attacked by the British that they jettisoned their bomb loads blindly and departed. The cathedral city of Canterbury was the geographical center of this fighting. On the right flank, roughly 140 miles to the west near St. Alban's Head, three squadrons from No. 10 Group had come to the support of No. 11 Group. Again the Germans pressed their attack home with the utmost courage.

"I saw them coming in, very even and tight in their formations," one observer wrote, "and then suddenly the formations disintegrated and you could see other planes, ours, I think, darting down from above and still others that seemed to come from nowhere attacking the leading German planes. The sound of the machine guns was very faint, like someone a long distance away drawing a stick across railings."

Some of the German bombers got through but only at Andover did they do much damage to the airfield. And this field was not in Fighter Command. As the invaders withdrew they were pursued and caught by elements of five squadrons.

All told the Luftwaffe flew 1,485 sorties, day and night, on Eagle Day compared with 727 by Fighter Command. The Germans lost a total of thirty-nine aircraft to the British defenders. This was accomplished for the loss of thirteen British planes and seven pilots. But it is not only on the basis of these figures that Eagle Day must be accounted a failure from the German standpoint. The German intelligence was poor. The Luftwaffe attacked eleven British airfields but only one of these was used by Fighter Command. As we have seen, the High Command allowed bombers to venture over Britain unescorted. The unwieldy Me 110's flew futile missions. Some damage was done by bombing around Southampton and near Detling. But considering the amount of time and effort put into Eagle Day the actual results were far from satisfactory.

The day's operations had yet another adverse effect from the German side. Apparently the German pilots' claims were even more exaggerated than those on the British side. General Otto Stapf of the Luftwaffe, who a month before had predicted it would take between two and four weeks to smash Fighter Command, now gave a wildly optimistic account of the operations to General Halder. Halder wrote in his diary that eight major British airbases had been virtually destroyed and that the ratio of German to British losses was one to three in all types of aircraft, one to five for fighters. Apparently these claims were accepted as trustworthy by the senior German commanders. From their standpoint the air offensive had begun with a resounding success. A note of false optimism pervaded staff discussions. For another two weeks the German view of the battle was unreal.

Although British morale bounded upward as a result of the fighting of August 13, it had a slightly firmer basis in fact. The *Times* editorial of August 14 said: "The facts, tested and trustworthy, are plain. Day after day our airmen, outnumbered as they generally are, strike down two or three times as many of their adversaries' machines as they lose of their own. . . ." This was an accurate assessment of Eagle Day.

Although heartened by their success on August 13, the pilots, staffs and commanders of Fighter Command knew that their trials had only begun. They had been fighting then for almost a month but they realized that the Luftwaffe had exerted maximum pressure only on that one day. Fortunately the German attacks on the 14th were on a smaller scale. Again airfields were the main targets and three were attacked effectively. At only one of these was the damage serious. Seventeen Germans were shot down, the RAF lost eight fighters. But even this relatively small loss was important to Fighter Command. The reserves of both pilots and aircraft were dwindling—Britain produced only 476 fighters that month—and the word "attrition" began to figure in the thinking of the watchers in Washington pessimistically calculating the islanders' chances of victory.

The German High Command in the person of Goering himself took measures to intensify the attacks. The Reichsmarschall was a braggart and a bully but no fool. He may have scented something wrong in the optimistic reports. At any rate he suggested a higher ratio of fighter protection, especially for dive bombers, and urged heavier attacks on RAF installations. But he did not know, and apparently his intelligence officers could not tell him, which airfields were used by Fighter Command. Nor did he appear greatly interested in further attacks on radar stations on which the whole British defense rested. Indeed the German intelligence service, pictured at the time, I recall, as ubiquitous and efficient, seems to have cut a sorry figure all through this phase of the battle. For they apparently believed that the strong resistance encountered by the German squadrons over southern England meant that the north had been denuded of fighter protection. This was a misjudgment for which the Germans paid heavily on August 15, which many people regard as a climax of the battle.

On that day, for the first and only time, the Luftwaffe

employed not only Luftflotten II and III in France, Belgium and Holland but Luftflotte V stationed in Norway. A total of 1,786 sorties were flown by the Luftwaffe. Goering threw everything into the battle. The thrust from Norway, predicated on the false assumption that the British fighters in the north had been drawn south by German pressure, was expected to attack both the airfields in the north and the industrial area along the Tyne.

The first German attack that day, however, was directed at Kent, possibly as a feint to divert attention from the north. Forty-five bombers escorted by fighters heavily damaged the airfield at Lympne and did some minor damage at Hawkinge. There was other German activity that morning in No. 11 Group's sector but no important engagements were reported.

No. 13 Group defended the north, under the command of Air Vice-Marshal Richard E. Saul. During the preceding days its pilots had felt slightly out of the war as the reports appeared of the major battles to the south. Now they were to be tested. Just after noon that day the Operations Room at No. 13 near Newcastle-on-Tyne reported the approach of twenty or more German aircraft about a hundred miles east of the Firth of Forth. Three squadrons of Spitfires and one of Hurricanes rose to meet the invaders, who, it soon developed, were far stronger than the original radar reports had estimated. In fact the Germans employed about a hundred Heinkel 111 bombers and seventy-five Me 110's. This was a major attack.

These odds worried the pilots of No. 13 Group no more

than they did their comrades to the south. The defending fighters attacked at once. The Spitfires of 72 Squadron, diving out of the sun from about 3,000 feet above the Me 110's, engaged the fighters with one formation while the remainder of the squadron attacked the bombers. These were routine tactics. The results were far from routine. The German bomber force apparently was taken by surprise. Some bombers dropped their bombs immediately. Others flew into clouds away from persistent Spitfires. The Me 110's, possibly because of the long range, had made the sortie without their rear gunners. According to Collier, they "were powerless to do anything but form defensive circles for their own protection and could only leave their charges to their own devices."

The German formation was now split and disorganized. One formation turned south, to be attacked by two more squadrons of British fighters. Heavily engaged by the Spitfires and Hurricanes and shaken by heavy antiaircraft fire from the batteries guarding the industrial area of the Tyne the Germans dropped their bombs almost blindly and returned to their base at Stavanger in Norway. The other formation, turning to the north, had no better luck. After its hot reception from 72 Squadron it encountered a second Spitfire squadron. This engaged the Me 110's and the Heinkel bombers in turn, forcing the latter to unload aimlessly with most of the bombs falling into the sea. The Germans, roughly handled, then turned for home. These attacks, incidentally, are one of the few instances where the bomber crews failed to push their attack home with all the tenacity and courage of the German race. It must be remembered that the crews were new to the job; this was their first taste of Fighter Command in this battle. But the engagements supported the belief of most squadron leaders and their pilots that once the German operational plan was upset by the defenders, as happened in this case when the main formation was split, the Luftwaffe formation deteriorated.

Luftflotte V had one more shot in the locker. At about the same time about fifty Junkers 88's, the fastest and most maneuverable of the German bombers, rose from their bases in Denmark and headed for Yorkshire. They were unescorted by fighters, a command decision that was soon proved tragically wrong. This attack brought No. 12 Group into the front line. With the help of No. 13 Group, in the form of a squadron of Blenheims, the British got four squadrons into the air, including one Spitfire and one Hurricane squadron. The Spitfires drew first blood.

The Ju 88's, though fast, were not fast enough for the Spits. They hunted and found cloud cover. When they crossed the coast they encountered a Hurricane flight that engaged them as they went inland. Despite these attacks by vastly superior fighters, the Germans pushed onward finding and bombing the airfield at Driffield. Unfortunately for their plan, which called for the elimination of Fighter Command bases, this was a Bomber Command station. The German bombs also hit, apparently luckily, an ammunition dump nearby. Nevertheless, the achievement of the Germans in pressing home their attacks in the face of qualitatively superior forces—the Spitfires and Hurricanes—was a remarkable one. They got away without further losses largely because the Blenheims were too slow to catch them.

From any standpoint the German attack from Scandinavian bases was a conclusive British victory. Aside from the damage to Driffield, the German bombers' operations had little or no effect on the Fighter Command. The minimum German loss was twenty-three aircraft. Fighter Command did not lose a plane or a man. General Stumpf in Norway, or possibly his superiors in Berlin, recognized the folly of further attacks. Never again in daylight did Luftflotte V join in the battle. It was apparent that without the support of single-engined fighters, the Me 109's, attacks on Britain from Norway and Denmark would be fruitless and costly.

By midafternoon, however, the invaders were attacking to the south in great strength. The airfield at Martlesham was successfully bombed although no less than seven British squadrons were ordered to intercept. An even larger force, about one hundred bombers escorted by fighters, simultaneously swept over eastern Kent. The British fighters, about forty in number, were engaged by the German escort while the bombers went on to bomb Rochester and the airfields at Eastchurch. From the German point of view this was a successful raid. The Luftwaffe lost only four or five fighters while the British lost nine and two aircraft factories were damaged at Rochester.

No. 11 Group, on whom the bulk of the fighting fell,

was now stretched to the limit. Pilots, those that were lucky, took off, fought, landed for fuel and ammunition and took off again. The Germans had attacked the north, they had twice hit the east coast, now they turned their attention to the south coast employing another large force, about seventy-five bombers and dive bombers plus single- and twin-engined fighters. "Where do the muckers come from?" one squadron leader asked that night. "They must make the bleeding aircraft overnight."

The attack on the south coast brought the fourth British group, No. 10, into the picture to reinforce No. 11's hard-pressed squadrons. The British concentrated on the right flank of No. 11's sector; risky business since the Luftwaffe might at any moment throw another attack at the left flank on the east coast.

The dive bombers, Ju 87's, were engaged as they neared Portland. Radar had given the British time to reach the best position, above and in the sun, and after punishing the Ju 87's they turned on the fighters. The Stukas dropped their bombs hurriedly and departed. At about the same time a formation of Hurricanes encountered about two squadrons of German bombers, unescorted, and engaged them. Another Hurricane squadron joined the fight but the Germans pushed on to bomb Middle Wallop airfield and a naval airdrome at Worthy Down. The latter attack was a failure. Seven of the fifteen attacking bombers were shot down and when the German intelligence officers reviewed the crews' stories that night they found that only three bombers had reached the target. At Middle Wallop the Germans were more successful. The ratio of losses was in favor of the British. They lost sixteen planes out of about 150 engaged, the largest force yet concentrated to meet a single attack. The Germans lost eight bombers, four dive bombers and thirteen Me 110's.

The British fighters were back on their bases when shortly after 6:00 P.M. the alarm was sounded again by radar. This time the attack was on No. 11 Group's left flank, with German formations headed for the airfields at Biggin Hill, Kenley and Redhill. Radar reported between sixty and seventy aircraft coming in and there was only one British squadron, No. 501, airborne. Such was the flexibility of the defense, however, that Air Vice-Marshal Park of No. 11 Group was able to add another eight and one-half squadrons to the defending forces. The pressure under which Fighter Command operated that day is shown by the fact that 501 Squadron had already been in action twice that day and had been in the air for some time when its Hurricanes made contact with the enemy. British resistance was determined, but the chances of war made this one of the most effective German attacks that day.

Driven off their original targets or perhaps mistaking targets in the confusion of a hundred encounters the Germans bombed the Croydon airfield and West Malling. Serious damage was done to both fields and two aircraft factories were hit at Croydon.

This was the last German daylight attack on that day although it should be remembered that all through this phase of the battle the Luftwaffe was busy at night attacking single targets or laying mines off the coast. The events of the 15th are a milestone on the British progress to victory. Their results affected the course of the battle thereafter.

The ratio of losses was a little better than two to one in favor of the RAF, which lost thirty-four aircraft to seventy-six Luftwaffe planes shot down. A high percentage of the German losses were bombers, which meant that the Luftwaffe lost not only the aircraft but a highly trained crew of three or four. The British, on the other hand, fighting over their own country, recovered those pilots who parachuted from their planes. I remember a squadron adjutant rushing out to tell an anxious squadron leader that "old Toby" had dropped into a vicarage garden and would be back with them that night. The squadron leader, commenting that the vicar would learn a lot of new words if he talked to Toby, returned to the wars.

The most important strategic result of the day was the withdrawal thereafter of Luftflotte V from the battle. Henceforth the fighting was to center over southern and southeastern England. This meant that aside from sporadic night raids the great industrial centers of the north were free from attack until that autumn.

Fed by intelligence based on pilots' reports even more optimistic than those of the British, the Germans, however, had no cause to be pessimistic. They calculated that the British had only about 300 fighters left in Fighter Command, whereas there were about 600 planes available. The RAF had lost about 200 fighters between July 10 and

August 15 but the Germans thought they had lost 500. The British were, however, extremely concerned over the growing shortage of experienced pilots. This was met by drawing volunteers from bomber and army cooperation squadrons and the formation of four new squadrons from among the Polish and Czechoslovakian airmen then in Britain.

Less evident but equally serious was the terrible fatigue of the surviving pilots. At the end of each day's operations they stumbled from their aircraft, drugged with weariness. They were young, they were strong, but they were flying three, four and five times a day. Fortunately for them it was on August 15, a day in which Fighter Command had flown well over nine hundred sorties, that Goering took a number of decisions of the utmost importance to the British cause.

The Reichsmarschall was not particularly happy about the course of the battle thus far although where the other services were concerned the Luftwaffe and its chief maintained a smiling confidence. On the 15th he summoned a conference of commanders, although one might have thought that on such an important day they should have been let alone to conduct the battle. As was true throughout the Battle of Britain, Goering's instructions were a mixture of sound direction and highly fallacious reasoning.

On the credit side must be placed his directive that until further orders the German operations were to be directed "exclusively" against the RAF, including the aircraft factories. "We must concentrate our efforts on the destruction of the enemy air forces," Goering continued. "Our night attacks are essentially dislocation raids, made so that the enemy defenses and population shall be allowed no respite; even these, however, should wherever possible be directed against air force targets." The Luftwaffe was warned not to waste time on shipping, especially British warships, or alternative targets whose destruction would not further the accomplishment of the primary objective.

These were sensible orders. But Goering added another instruction. He told his commanders it was "doubtful" whether there was any point in continuing to attack radar sites since thus far these raids had been fruitless. Actually one station on the Isle of Wight had been virtually destroyed. Fortunately the Germans did not know this. The Reichsmarschall's instruction was tentative in nature. Yet the Germans made only two more attacks on radar stations. As we have seen, the German High Command on the whole had little respect for radar. Yet by this time harried Luftwaffe officers were already complaining that, although briefed before an operation on the impossibility of British interception over the assigned target, they invariably found their path beset by Spitfires and Hurricanes from the time they crossed the coast and, in some cases, even earlier. The decision to break off the attacks on the radar stations must be considered a major error on the part of the Reichsmarschall and his staff.

The great effort on August 15 exhausted the Luftwaffe almost as much as it did the RAF, despite the former's superiority in numbers. Nevertheless, the attacks on the next day were heavy although, it seemed to the British, they were pressed with less resolution. The Germans flew nearly 1,700 sorties and heavily damaged the airfield at Tangmere. Again the ratio of losses was better than two to one in favor of the British, forty-five Germans down for a loss of twenty-one British planes. The 17th was a quiet day but on August 18 the Luftwaffe returned to make a series of heavy attacks on eight airfields and one radar station, that at Poling in Sussex. It was a costly day for the Luftwaffe, which lost seventy-one aircraft to twenty-seven for the RAF. But the station at Poling remained out of action for the remainder of August, a serious handicap to Fighter Command. It was the last radar station to be attacked during the battle.

We have been watching the conflict unfold on the big screen: from the Tyne in the north to Portland in the southwest. Let us return to 85 Squadron and its Hurricanes on August 18. It was not a very famous squadron and August 18 was not one of the "big" days. But what the squadron did on that day, and what it and many other squadrons like it did all the time, won the battle. Here is the log, unadorned, of that day's operations:

Debden 18/8/40—At 17:24 hours the squadron composed of thirteen AC [aircraft] was ordered to patrol Debden home base at 10,000 ft. At 17:30 they were airborne and immediately ordered to intercept Raid 51 which was crossing coast in vicinity of Folkestone, and at 17:39 when 8 miles NE of Chelmsford S/L Townsend sighted E/A approx. 15 miles east of him.

The squadron set a course E to attack. The enemy consisted of a number of aircraft estimated at between 150 and 350 machines. At the time these were approaching in very rough Vic formation stepped up from 10,000 feet to 18,000 ft.

The lower advanced tier comprising Ju 87's followed by He 111's 2,000 feet higher. Still higher up were Ju 88's and Me 110's at approximately 15,000 feet with Me 109's at approx. 17,000 feet. On sighting the squadron the enemy employed the following tactics:

a) The two lower tiers composed of Ju 87's and He 111's immediately turned seawards; b) the three higher formations of Ju 88's, Me 110's and Me 109's started to climb steeply, while turning sharply from left to right continuously, eventually forming two circles. The Ju 88's which were numerically small climbed with the 110's and formed one circle turning anti-clockwise at approximately 18,000 feet and the Me 109's at 20,000 feet, their circle also being anti-clockwise. Owing to the numerical superiority of the enemy the squadron was unable to deliver any set methods of attack and the battle developed into individual dog fights. The main action took place at approx. 8 to 12 miles east of Foulness Pt.

S/L Townsend attacked one Me 110 with full deflection shot, three second burst whilst doing a left hand turn and the enemy aircraft heeled over spiralling vertically downwards out of control from 10,000 feet.

PO English and Sergeant Howes saw it go down and corroborate the opinion that the pilot must have been killed.

He then attacked a Me 109 and EA caught fire after a three second burst and spun down in flames. He was then attacked by another Me 109 but without difficulty manoeuvred on its tail. Pilot baled out and machine broke up in air. He then attacked another Me 109 ineffectually and then with ammunition exhausted returned to Debden.

P/O English (Red 2) followed S/L Townsend in the attack

on 20 Me 110's and tackled an Me 110 which dived ahead of him. He gave it one long burst, saw tracer entering the wing and silenced the rear gunner.

Sgt. Howes (Red 3) while Red 1 and 2 were attacking climbed to 9,000 feet and attacked an Me 110 and saw it crash into water. He then climbed and made a No. 2 attack on one of several 110's circling which burst into flames. He then climbed to 15,000 feet and tackled a straggling Do 17 which went down out of sight with thick smoke trailing from it. F/L Hamilton (Yellow 1) attacked a He 111, with a five second burst and on breaking away it dropped its undercarriage, smoke pouring from the fuselage and two engines and went gliding slowly down to sea. He then attacked a Me 110 which dived down with both engines on fire.

P/O Marshall (Yellow 2) followed Yellow 1 in pursuit of the Me 110 but broke away to engage a He 111 three miles away and opened fire at 250 yards. Pieces broke away from the AC which was in a cloud of white vapour and flying into P/O Marshall's starboard wing cut off the tail unit of the EA. Despite a damaged aircraft minus a wing tip he managed to land safely at Debden. Sgt. Ellis (Yellow 3) destroyed a Me 109 and damaged one Me 110. He used his cinecamera gun throughout the combat.

Sgt Walker Smith (Blue 3) delivered a frontal attack on a Me 110, 150 yards above it. The EA glided down from 8,000 feet to hit the sea 40 miles out. After firing several ineffectual bursts at another AC he made a similar frontal attack. This time the Me 110 broke up, one of the crew baling out into the sea.

P/O Hodgson (Blue 4) during the dog fight climbed to 12,000 feet and dived on a Do 17 which went diving down white smoke pouring from its engines. He then turned on the tail of a Me 109 by a steep climbing turn and after a short burst the EA went diving vertically into the sea. He then climbed to 20,000 feet to a circle of Me 110's, made a snap shot at one and then dived on another making its starboard engine smoke.

P/O Gowers (Green 1) attacked a Ju 87 from dead astern with a five second burst, followed by a seven second burst and the EA was almost completely blotted out by black smoke and dived towards the sea. P/O Lockhard (Green 2) attacked an Me 110 and silenced the rear gunner.

P/O Lewis D.F.C. (Green 3) encountered 12 Me 110's circling at 18,000 feet one of which proceeded to dive at a Hurricane down below and in so doing presented a plain view on the sights at 150 yards. Two short bursts caused it to smoke and dive at a steep angle.

P/O Hemingway (Blue 2) followed F/L Lee D.S.O., D.F.C. (Blue 1) who chased a Ju 88 but broke away to attack a circling formation of Ju 88's. Hemingway attacked a Ju 88 and was himself attacked by two Ju 88's in close formation. His engine was hit, his cockpit filled with oil and glycol and his AC went into a spin. He pulled out at 7,000 feet and set course for land but his engine stopped and he had to bale out. After being 1½ hours in the sea he was picked up by Lightship 81 boat, 12 miles E of Clacton. He was then landed at Felixstowe by M.T.B. (motor torpedo boat) and returned to Debden the next day.

F/L Lee D.S.O., D.F.C. (Blue 1) was last seen by S/L Townsend D.F.C. and F/O Gowers, 10 miles NE of Foulness Point chasing 3 Me 110's well ahead of him. He failed to return to Debden and was reported missing.

Enemy Casualties
6 Me 110's, 3 Me 109's, 1 He 111 destroyed.
1 He 111, 1 Me 110, 1 Ju 87, 1 Me 109 probably destroyed.
4 Me 110's, 2 Do 17's damaged.
Our Casualties.

F/L R. H. A. Lee D.S.O., D.F.C. and his Hurricane missing.
1 Hurricane destroyed. 1 Hurricane damaged.

All the pilots agreed that the enemy were disinclined to
make combat and in this action the Me 109 and Me 110 proved
extremely easy to overcome.

That was August 18 for 85 Squadron. A good day sad-
dened by the loss of Dickie Lee. They thought for a long
time in the squadron that he would return. But he never
did. For many people Lee was an integral part of that
first year of the war; the first desperate, explosive encounter with the Germans. Other pilots came, brave men, good
fellows, but they never quite replaced the people like Lee
who were killed that summer.

The weather worsened on the 19th and heavy cloud
continued through August 23. There were some German
attacks, never in great strength. On both sides the commands assessed the results of the first phase of the battle
and planned for the next while the fighting men rested, or
at least came as near resting as was possible in the
circumstances.

At this point, indeed almost until the end, the Germans
retained the tactical initiative. They still outnumbered the
British although the difference in strength was not so out-
rageous as they concluded on the basis of their intelligence
reports. They still had the chance of overwhelming Fighter
Command and the orders given by Goering that day were
intended to do just that. Luftflotte V was pulled out of the
day battle and ordered to prepare for a heavy raid on
Glasgow at night. Luftflotten II and III were to continue

to wear down the RAF and every ruse was to be used to bring Fighter Command to battle. Bombers were to be used sparingly; their role was to be that of decoys enticing the British Fighters to battle. The German flying tactics also were altered. Originally they had flown in with bombers low and fighters high. The British had met this sort of attack by sending one formation of fighters against the German bombers while a second formation engaged the enemy fighters. These British tactics had been especially effective on the 15th; the Germans soon altered their formations. Now these were to be much tighter, with fighters ahead, on the wings, and just above the bombers. This was a harder nut to crack.

At about this time, too, the Luftwaffe withdrew the Ju 87's from the battle. They had proved far too vulnerable to the British fighters. They now settled on the airfields of the Pas de Calais to wait for the day when, unworried by British fighters, they would hammer the British defenses against invasion and any ships of the Royal Navy that ventured into the Channel. Indeed the first phase of the Battle of Britain marked the beginning of the end of the Stuka as an effective weapon. It reappeared briefly in the Balkans and in Russia the next year and it was of some use in the early fighting in Africa, but as Allied fighter strength grew the Stuka, which had spread terror throughout Poland and France, became obsolete.

Goering's orders after the conference at Karinhall on August 19 were clear. And it is clear too that whatever dreams of easy conquest Hitler may have enjoyed at that time, the Reichsmarschall understood that this was a critical moment.

"We have reached the decisive period of the air war against England," Goering said. "The vital task is to turn all means at our disposal to the defeat of the enemy air force. Our first aim is the destruction of the enemy's fighters. If they no longer take the air, we shall attack them on the ground or force them into battle by directing bomber attacks against targets within range of our fighters. At the same time and on a growing scale, we must continue our activities against the ground organization of the enemy bomber units. Surprise attacks on the enemy aircraft industry must be made by day and by night. Once the enemy air force has been annihilated, our attacks will be directed as ordered against other vital targets."

On the German airdromes, among the men who were directing and leading the offensive, it had become clear during the fighting from August 13 onward that Fighter Command could not be crippled by striking at forward airfields only. They knew that, after radar, the flexible system of control was the greatest organizational advantage possessed by the British. By July, Adolf Galland recalled later, "we realized that the RAF fighter formations must be controlled by some new procedure because we heard commands skillfully and accurately directing Spitfires and Hurricanes on to German formations. We had no fighter control at the time and no way of knowing what the British were doing with their forces as each battle progressed. As a result each German formation had to fly where it was ordered according to a carefully prearranged battle plan and had to depend on its own observations and initiative to assess the British reaction and take offensive measures. The planning aimed at as much variety as possible to confuse Fighter Command with the hope, too, that some successful strategy might be hit upon by chance."

Since the Germans invariably encountered more aircraft over southeast England (No. 11 Group) than elsewhere, the operational commanders decided to concentrate their attacks on this area. Like the majority of commanders they were optimistic. This time the Luftwaffe would strike deep inland and destroy the major airfields. This time the British control system would be dislocated and ultimately destroyed. This time the British as well as the Germans would be flying blind. No slip-ups. No more unescorted bombers. This time it would be different.

During this period the Luftwaffe's manipulation of figures of German and British losses increased. The victims of this deception were enlarged, however. The Luftwaffe not only lied to the German people. It began to lie to the army, whose high command was anxiously awaiting news that the RAF had been driven from the skies—as promised—and that the invasion could proceed. The Luftwaffe had lost 602 planes between August 8 and August 26. But Halder was told by the air generals that the figure was 353. Goering claimed the destruction of 791 British fighters. The RAF had lost 259 during this period.

The British, of course, were not rich in planes or pilots. But by the end of the first phase they had about 161 Spitfires and Hurricanes available for immediate transfer to squadrons. Pilots were very tired, too many of the veterans were dead, and the next big intake of trained pilots could not be expected until the middle of September.

Morale, however, was very high. "I don't think we thought much about what the war was about and how it was going," Max Aitken recalled twenty years later. "There was always a job to do that day. Losing? No, I don't think any of us ever thought we could lose the battle or the war. It just didn't enter our heads."

For the pilots of Fighter Command the Battle of Britain was their individual war, just as the officers and men of the destroyers, frigates and corvettes of the Royal Navy considered the Battle of the Atlantic as *their* war. Even Aitken, then a fighter pilot—he had joined the Royal Auxiliary Air Force in 1935—saw it that way. Yet he had better cause than most to see the war as a whole. His father was Lord Beaverbrook, the Minister for Aircraft Production; one of the dynamos installed by Churchill to accelerate the war effort.

To Aitken and the other survivors of the battle nothing that followed in the war can ever eclipse the stark and shining memories of those summer days. He went on to command a night fighter squadron and rose to the rank of group captain, winning a Distinguished Flying Cross and a Distinguished Service Order in the process. But for him and for many others the war is still "that summer." He is now chairman of the board of Beaverbrook Newspapers Ltd. When he sits in his office above the rattle of Fleet

Street and talks of those days the listener is taken with him to other, less imposing buildings where young men in uniform lounged and talked while they waited for orders to fly and fight.

The figures of German and British losses and victories known to the public in the United Kingdom helped maintain the morale of the people. There was no undue optimism but for the first time since the war began the man in the street had something to crow about. Besides, the prophets had told him that the outbreak of war would mean terrible air raids on London. Well, the war was nearly a year old and, although some bombs had fallen, London was almost untouched. Meanwhile the weather was clear and warm, everyone said the army was getting more arms and "the old man"—as Churchill was already known in the bus queues—had told them that all they had to do was stick it; which meant hard work and the surrender of many of the pleasanter things of life. This they were willing to do. Through that summer one could almost feel the growth of a consciousness of their role in the war and what it meant; the shame of Munich was replaced by a determined pride and a resolute purpose. Since they were British, this rarely appeared in ordinary conversation. But it was the best possible preparation for a country that in the coming months would have to undergo the long ordeal of bombing.

This sort of public sentiment is difficult to report in tangible terms. It was poorly understood in Washington, where, during the first phase of the battle, an uneasy skepticism about Britain's chances of survival prevailed. "The Ambassador in London, Joseph P. Kennedy, had steadily foreseen the downfall of Britain since the Nazis marched into Poland," Forrest Davis and Ernest K. Lindley reported in *How War Came to America*. On the part of the military this skepticism was the result of the rather exaggerated opinion of the Luftwaffe and the German army held by the army and the Army Air Force. Generally, however, neither the politicians nor the generals and admirals realized how much a high morale counts in such a situation. The soldiers thought the British were "through." Six weeks, they said, would see the job done. You had to hand it to the Krauts, they knew how to fight a war. They were wrong then and they were wrong a year later when the Germans attacked Russia—the Soviet Union also was given six weeks by the big brass—and the memory of these gross misjudgments is not particularly reassuring to anyone now inquiring for information at the font of military wisdom.

So the first phase came to an end. The British, although shaken, were still there. Across the Channel the Germans gathered themselves for the start of Act II. The battle was still in the balance.

Chapter VII

The fortunes of war flow this way and that, and no prudent fighter holds his enemy in contempt.

—GOETHE

The Germans were not the only ones to ponder over the results and tactics in the first phase of the battle. The British had been doing some hard thinking of their own. They were convinced that as long as the sector stations that controlled the battle survived then, other things being equal, they would whip the Luftwaffe. The only German planes that could damage the sector stations were the bombers. Consequently, Fighter Command must concentrate on the bombers when its fighters intercepted German attacks. Moreover, when the Germans mounted an attack against one of the key stations, then British fighters must patrol the area to meet the bombers.

Operationally the new British directive, which emerged from this high-level thinking, called for the concentration of both Spitfires and Hurricanes on the German bombers. But, as we know from the preceding chapter, the Germans intended to tie their fighters very closely to the bomber formations. When the battle resumed the RAF found that in many cases the interceptors returned to the familiar tactics in which the Spitfire sought out the German fighter cover and the Hurricanes went for the bombers.

By the time the second phase of the battle opened the Germans had decided to withdraw Luftflotte V from daylight operations against Britain. But we must remember that in this period of maximum strain the British didn't know it. Consequently, despite the enormous pressure exerted by the Luftwaffe, the British did not dare weaken the strength of No. 13 Group in the north by using its squadrons to reinforce the other groups. The burden still rested on No. 11 Group. Now, after almost three months of action, it was beginning to feel the strain. The veteran squadrons contained an increasing number of new pilots recently graduated from training units. About a third of the remaining squadrons were new to the group. They had been exchanged for other veteran squadrons whose losses and fatigue made rest advisable.

The pause between August 18 and August 24 benefited both sides. Seen from this distance in time, however, the British in the long run made the most out of it. Their tactical reappraisal seems a little more acute, more in line with the known facts. But, more important than that, Fighter Command had a chance to catch its breath. Flying was a more difficult business then than it is now; the German bombers and fighters used navigational aids rudimentary by modern standards. Yet if the Germans believed they were beating the RAF their decision to give the British a five-day rest is difficult to understand.

To an increasingly proud Britain, understanding came easily. The fighter pilots had fought the Germans to a standstill. Arising in the House of Commons after a visit to several fighter stations during which he had been so deeply moved he said not a word during the return journey, Winston Churchill paid Fighter Command the finest compliment any service knows. The *Times* proclaimed that the "supremacy of our airmen is now triumphantly proved."

The world rolled on. Enthusiasts reported that amateur dramatics were stimulated by the air attacks that had become customary, almost routine throughout England's southeast corner. A new picture of Princess Margaret appeared on her tenth birthday. *The Chocolate Soldier* was revived. People who for years had spent holidays "abroad," i.e., in Europe, now tramped through the Lake District or tasted the dubious pleasures of the more genteel seaside resorts. It was not much of a year for bathing, although the weather was warm and bright. The appearance of towns on east and southern coasts began to change as a result of the army's labors. Subalterns with artistic leanings found their métier in disguising pillboxes as public toilets or newspaper stands and the mechanically minded evolved unofficial but horrible mechanisms for dealing with the invading Germans. For everyone was sure they were coming.

The Germans did what they could to maintain this belief. On August 21 they began to shell Dover from their positions around Calais. "Better Aim Likely with Practice," the *Times* headline reported. There had been just enough bombing in the preceding weeks to father the first crop of bomb stories, a scanty yield compared with what came after the major attacks on London began, and amateur statisticians in pubs were ready to work out the chances of being hit by a bomb. The British, however, maintained their interests in other values connected with the war. There was considerable relief when Sir John Anderson announced the release of a substantial number of enemy aliens interned earlier. The death of Leon Trotsky was noted by the editorial writers. But there was a curious absence of news from Europe. The Continent lay quiet under the heavy hand of the Germans. To be sure, propaganda poured from Berlin and in Vichy the government of Marshal Pétain was busy arraigning its former allies for various crimes. But of the people of Europe little was known. For allies and friends Britain looked toward the Empire and to the United States. The British were very much alone.

As the second phase of the battle opened the importance of the sector stations was reorganized by both the attackers and the defenders. These stations were the centers for operational control of the squadrons, once Group Headquarters had ordered the planes into the air. There were seven such stations in No. 11 Group, each of them usually controlling up to three squadrons, located at Tangmere on the South Downs, Debden, home of our friends in 85 Squadron, Kenley, near Caterham, Biggin Hill, which guarded the southern air approaches to London,

Hornchurch near Dagenham, an industrial area, North Weald near Epping Forest and, finally, Northolt west of London.

These seven stations with their airfields held the keys to victory or defeat. In all wars, at all times there have been certain positions, unremarkable usually in terms of intrinsic value, whose possession has been vital: men have fought for a mountain defile, a castle keep, a bridge, a riverbank, a ridge. Now they flew high to defend these seven stations and in the stations men and women, for the Women's Auxiliary Air Force was there too, went about their business like dedicated clerks. They had little in common with those who in other wars had held similar positions of the utmost importance for their courage did not demand hot-blooded exchanges with a seen foe but long hours of brain work at the utmost pressure while outside the antiaircraft guns barked and occasionally there came the whistle and rumbling roar of exploding bombs nearby. With the pilots in the air above they were part of the Fighter Command. In their stubborn resolution to keep going whatever befell they were not unworthy of the young men whose efforts they directed.

The Germans began the second phase of the battle with deliberation. On the morning of August 24 four or five forays by the Luftwaffe kept the defenders busy without bringing about a major engagement. Then, just after noon, they struck hard and quickly at Manston, one of the forward airbases. But the attack had been preceded by further feints, the Germans were boxing carefully, and it caught three quarters of the squadron guarding the Manston airfield on the ground refueling. Meeting very little opposition on the way in, the German formation bombed the field heavily, so heavily that the squadron based there and most of the ground staff had to be withdrawn to another field. Against this success, however, the Luftwaffe had to count the losses resulting from a brisk engagement after the raid. Encountering first the full squadron of Defiants stationed at Manston—the nine aircraft fueling, when the attack began, got into the air amidst falling bombs—and a squadron of Hurricanes the Germans lost five bombers and two fighters. Manston, of course, was not a sector station. Although the RAF was driven from it by this attack, the Luftwaffe had to go deeper into England before it could achieve its objective of smashing the nerve system of Fighter Command.

The Germans' combination of feints and genuine attacks came close to putting No. 11 Group off balance that day. Three hours later when a Luftwaffe force of about fifty aircraft made a second attack on Manston, the British had four squadrons in the air. But half of these were nearing the end of their fuel and were of little help. While Manston was being pounded for the second time, another German formation headed for Hornchurch, one of the sector stations. There luck was with the Germans. But it was not enough.

The Defiants of 264 Squadron which had been at Manston during the day's first raid were again caught on the ground at Hornchurch. Despite the bombing, seven of them managed to take off and engage the Germans. While they were climbing the antiaircraft fire began to come uncomfortably close. Consequently the attack was less damaging than might have been expected. Only a fraction of the bombs dropped hit the airfield.

The battle now shifted to North Weald, another sector station. British fighters were there to engage the Germans but the latter's new tactics paid. The RAF pilots found it extremely difficult to get to the bombers through the German fighter escort and the bombers did considerable damage to the station. At the end of the attack North Weald still exercised control of its squadrons, but only just. The British had knocked down five bombers and four fighters. But they had lost eight precious fighters although five of the pilots were unharmed. Given the Luftwaffe's numerical superiority, a loss ratio of nine to eight throughout the battle meant defeat for the English.

The day of misfortune was not over. Again a series of German feints confused the defenders. Again about fifty bombers heavily escorted by fighters got through this time to Portsmouth. There were four squadrons in the neighborhood of the great naval base but only one of these succeeded in engaging the Germans. But it was in a poor position from which to attack, nearly a thousand feet below the enemy, and the bombers hammered Portsmouth and its dockyard, doing considerable damage and killing more than a hundred people. This attack, mounted by Luftflotte III, was one of that organization's last major daylight operations.

Although the British shot down thirty-six German planes that day and lost twenty-two of their own, the advantage lay with the attackers. Owing to confusion in assessing the radar sightings, to which the German feints contributed, No. 11 Group found it hard to intercept and engage the incoming formations before they attacked the targets. The new tactics of close fighter escort made it difficult to get at the bombers. The day's operations thus began a period of maximum stress for the British.

The night of August 24–25 was notable for a sudden increase in the scale of German bombing. These raids ranged from Tyneside in the north to Swansea in the west. The center of London got its first taste of bombing. Aside from one bomber airfield damaged the purely military damage was negligible. But the Battle of Britain had now become a national operation. Primarily the country depended upon Fighter Command. The command could operate at maximum efficiency only if it had the necessary communications and supplies and if its personnel were alert. German night bombing thus played a small part in the battle by tiring and disrupting the defense.

The Germans reinvested in success on the next day. All through that morning the radar reported concentrations behind the French coast and Fighter Command flew a number of futile patrols. But the main attack, the only one that day, was not launched until late afternoon. Again a compact force of forty-five bombers was protected by well over a hundred fighters. Again the target was an airdrome, Warmwell in No. 10 Group's sector. Again the three squadrons concentrated by the defense were too few in number. The German bombers got a straight run for the target and knocked Warmwell out for eighteen hours. Try as they might, the British fighters couldn't get through the fighter screen. They shot down only one bomber but got eleven fighters, losing eleven fighters of their own. Again the ratio of losses in the long run favored the quantitatively superior Luftwaffe twelve to eleven. Later a snap attack that ended in a dog fight near Dover cost the Germans eight more aircraft. But the British lost an additional five fighters.

On the 26th the Germans maintained the pressure on the sector stations and fighter airfields. Debden, Hornchurch and North Weald were the targets but only Debden was seriously damaged. The pilots of 85 Squadron, now flying from Croydon, saw action that day. Let the log tell the story:

Croydon 26/8/40—Twelve Hurricanes of 85 Squadron took off at 14:49 hrs to patrol base and were then vectored to the Maidstone area. At 15:20 hrs near Eastchurch 15 Dornier 215's were sighted flying in stepped up Vic formation at 15,000 ft and escorted by approx 30 Me 109's which were flying at 5,000 to 10,000 feet higher. The Squadron executed a head-on attack at the Dorniers and the leading section of E/A broke away from formation. This section was followed by several Hurricanes, the remainder of E/A having turned back in a S.E. direction. The engagement became general and three Dornier 215's were definitely destroyed by the Squadron as a whole who nearly all contributed.

One Dornier 215 after a series of astern and quarter attacks was seen to go down in low diving left hand turns with starboard engine stopped.

The second Dornier broke away after repeated attacks and made out to sea on port motor only, but apparently thought the better of it as pieces were falling from it, because it turned back and pancaked 1-2 miles due E of Eastchurch. The third Dornier was seen to disappear in clouds losing height. It was then encountered by Sgt. Howes who finished it off with the remainder of his ammunition. The crash was also witnessed by P/O Allard. Those taking part in this engagement were S/L Townsend, F/Lt Hamilton, P/O Hemingway, P/O Worrall, P/O Allard, Sgt. Howes, P/O English, P/O Hodgson, Sgt. Walker-Smith, Sgt. Ellis, F/O Woods-Scawn and F/O Gowers.

F/O Woods-Scawn attacked a Me 109 while climbing, firing three second bursts into its belly. He saw bits flying off in all directions and E/A appeared to whipstall, but he was unable to see if it crashed as he had to dive away.

P/O Hemingway, after the general engagement with the Dorniers, was climbing to engage some Me 109's when he was hit behind the cockpit and in the engine by cannon shell. As the engine became red-hot and it was impossible to remain in the A/C he baled out and landed safely in Pitsea Marshes. The Dornier 215's were painted light blue beneath the wings except one which was black.

Enemy casualties: 3 Do 215 destroyed
1 ME 109 probable
Our casualties: 1 Hurricane destroyed

The fighting elsewhere that day was not satisfactory for the British. Two squadrons saw the German formation approach Debden but once again they could not force a way through the fighters to attack the bombers. A third squadron dispatched from the Midlands (No. 12 Group) arrived too late to be of much help. Only when the Luftwaffe struck again at Portsmouth did the British restore the balance.

This time No. 11 Group concentrated three squadrons of fighters. These harried the German formations on their route to the naval base, forcing the bombers to loose their loads before they got to the navy dockyard. Seven German aircraft were destroyed, bringing the day's bag to forty-one including nineteen bombers. Fighter Command lost thirty-one aircraft and sixteen pilots.

The ratio of losses had tipped temporarily in favor of the British. Yet the losses to Fighter Command were extremely serious. Short of fighters and short of pilots, the loss of a single plane, the death or wounding of one pilot represented an important setback to the RAF. From now until September 7 the command was hanging on. The pilots themselves seemed unaffected by the situation. Slouching in flying kit as they pursued the *Daily Mirror's* "Jane" through her adventures, they were as confident as ever. But in those days the terrible fatigue, the cumulative tiredness of weeks and months of constant effort marked young faces. Friendship ran strong in the squadrons.

"You go through training with a chap, you rip about on leave with him, you get the same feeling you have about yourself—they won't get me. Then they do get him. You want to get the mugger that got him or someone like him. But you feel there's a gap somewhere. Something's missing." Thus a pilot one night at Biggin Hill when we stood together in the starlight and listened to the beat of a German motor in the darkness above.

On the 27th, Fighter Command instituted a new command tactic. Pilots leading formations were instructed on sighting the enemy to send a "Tallyho!" message giving the numbers, position, height and course of the raiders. This, it was hoped, would enable the defenders to concentrate more rapidly against the enemy forces and reduce the disparity in numbers. The introduction of a cry from the hunting field into a life-and-death struggle was very British. And the pilots' rendition of the cry was typical of the command. "Tallyho!" I heard an excited voice call at a sector station headquarters, "there's a couple of dozen of the muckers and I'm going in."

"And a hell of a lot of use that information is to us," remarked the controller.

There was not much opportunity to try the new system that day. The Germans made few attacks although they lost nine planes to one for the RAF. But on August 28 the pressure on the airdromes and sector stations was renewed. Eastchurch and Rochford were the targets. Once again the British failed to halt the formation as it swept toward the target; the escorting fighters shooting down two British fighters and damaging four more in the attack on the Coastal Command station at Eastchurch. At Rochford the German fighters again smashed through the screen of defenders and the bombers went in to bomb the airfield although the damage was negligible. Still the Germans were getting through and inflicting serious losses on the defenders in the air and on ground targets. The day ended with twenty British losses to thirty German. And the offensive showed no signs of slackening.

Late that afternoon the Germans themselves tried something new. Strong fighter forces swept over East Kent at 25,000 feet in an attempt to lure Fighter Command to battle. The Hurricanes of 85 Squadron took off to meet them while a stout, familiar figure chewing a large cigar watched. While Mr. Churchill waited they fought a notable battle:

Croydon 28:8:40—Ten Hurricanes took off at 1602 hours to patrol Tenderden and were then ordered to intercept Raid 15. About 20 Me 109's were sighted at 1625 hours flying at 18,000 ft in the Dungeness area. One Me 110 was seen at the same time in the same vicinity.

The Squadron approached from the sun, but were spotted at the last moment by E/A who appeared not to be anxious to engage and broke formation in all directions. Six Me 109's were destroyed and 1 Me 110 damaged.

S/L Townsend gave a two-three second burst and E/A rolled over and dived steeply, seen going down by F/Lt Hamilton and P/O Gowers, both of whom saw black and white smoke coming out of E/A. S/L Townsend estimated his position at about 12 miles N.W. of Lympne. This confirmed by Maidstone Observer Corps who received a report at 1646 that a Me 109 had crash landed at R 5167, the pilot being taken prisoner. P/O Allard attacked E/A at 200 yds closing to 20 yards and it caught fire and dived vertically into the sea, two-three miles outside Folkestone harbour. Witnessed by P/O English. He then fired several short bursts from 250 yds at another Me 109 which was making for France. E/A dived and flew at 20 feet from sea but engine failed with black (smoke) coming out, position then was about 5 miles N of St. Inglevert, which was confirmed by 11 Group signal 11G/174 of 29/8. P/O Hodgson chased E/A from 17,000 ft down across the Channel to 20 ft above sea level. Fired several bursts and saw pieces falling off and only 1/3 of rudder left. E/A was going very slowly when last seen and emitting much black smoke. P/O Hodgson had to turn back when 5 miles NW of Cap Gris-Nez owing to lack of ammunition but he was certain that E/A was finished. This was confirmed by 11 Group signal 11G/174 of 29/8.

F/O Woods-Scawn attacked E/A from quarter following to astern and gave two long bursts. Black smoke and what appeared to be petrol from the wing tanks poured out of E/A and it dived down vertically. He followed it down for several thousand feet and left it when it was obviously out of control. It was believed to have crashed near Dungeness and this was confirmed by Maidstone Observer Corps who reported a Me 109 in the sea Dymchurch at 1640 hrs.

Sgt. Walker-Smith attacked Me 109 and the port petrol tank was seen to explode and then went into steep dive. At that moment Sgt. Walker-Smith was fired at and had to take evasive action but immediately afterwards dived and saw a large explosion on the sea and black smoke. P/O Hodgson confirmed having seen a Me 109 dive into the sea at this point. P/O Gowers attacked Me 110 from astern and saw [bullets?]* entering but it went into a shallow dive toward French coast and got away. P/O Gowers used all his ammunition and definitely damaged E/A.

The Me 109s all had Yellow Wing tips.

Enemy casualties: 6 Me 109's destroyed
                               1 Me 110 damaged

Our casualties: Nil

* Word unclear.

This action was watched by the Prime Minister during a visit to the SE coastal defences.

The reader will note that 85 Squadron did its utmost to verify enemy losses. Also that its Hurricanes, although considered by the high command better suited for attacks on bombers, continued to do well against Me 109's, the best fighter in the Luftwaffe at that time.

During this period of intensive daylight pressure Luft-flotte III had been preparing for a series of major attacks by night. These began on the night of August 28 and continued through the night of August 31–September 1. Into these attacks the Luftwaffe High Command threw not only the regular Junkers 88 and Heinkel 111 bomber but the Focke-Wulf 200's, an aircraft with an exceptional range for that day, previously used in the Battle of the Atlantic. Sensibly enough the Luftwaffe High Command wanted to hammer the great port of Liverpool and the industrial Midlands. They did do a good deal of damage and inflicted many casualties in Liverpool on the night of August 31. But the attacks generally were widely scattered, ranging from the Tyne in the north to Swansea in the west. The railroads on which the British fighting services then largely relied for supply and transport were unaffected by the raids.

After a quiet day on August 29 the Luftwaffe resumed the attack in strength on August 30. By midmorning it was clear that the sector stations of No. 11 Group were the enemy targets. Biggin Hill was Air Vice-Marshal Park's principal worry and the fighters from that station were ordered up to intercept the raiders. Once again the Germans got through. Biggin Hill was severely damaged. And, although the German force was caught as it flew homeward, the score was in favor of the Luftwaffe; six planes lost to eight for the British during the engagement.

The Germans were now directing a series of attacks on southeast England that kept the outnumbered British at a disadvantage. A force got through the fighters and bombed Luton, damaging the Vauxhall auto plant. A smaller formation slipped past the fighters and hit the Coastal Command station at Detling. Then another German force flying westward suddenly turned south and again bombed Biggin Hill, doing even more damage than in the earlier attack.

This time the German bombs killed sixty-five people on the station, damaged hangars, workshops and supply depots, and cut the gas and electricity lines. Considering the importance of the sector stations to the British, this was a major reverse. Yet on that day, August 30, Fighter Command flew 1,054 sorties by day, its maximum effort thus far in the battle, while the Luftwaffe flew 1,345 sorties by day; the largest German force employed since the middle of the month. The Germans lost thirty-six aircraft; the British twenty-six.

It was another good day for 85 Squadron as the log shows:

Croydon 30/8/40—Eleven Hurricanes took off at 10:36 hours and vectored on a course of 105 degrees to intercept various raids approaching coast. At 11.10 hours approximately 50 He

111's were sighted at 16,000 feet near Bethenden flying in sections of three in general mass, above these were large numbers of Me 109's in support. Estimated total of E/A about 150–200.

The Squadron went inland until well in front of Heinkels and then executed a head-on attack on them, diving from sun in four waves of three. [*sic*] This had the desired effect and the bomber formation was effectively dispersed, although in view of the nature of the attack and the rapidity with which it was carried out, it was quite impossible to see the extent of the damage inflicted at the time. A general dog-fight then ensued and numerous individual combats took place. It was noticed that the firing from E/A, in particular the Me 110's, was erratic and indiscriminate. Me 110 showed in this combat, and in preceding ones, a marked disinclination to go down lower than 16,000–18,000 ft. It was further noticed that the He 111 did not stand up to the head-on attack at all well, and that this form of attack was far more successful against them than against Dorniers a few days previously. S/L Townsend attacked Me 110, gave burst at 200 yds range and E/A last seen 20 miles S. of Beachy Head with black smoke coming from port engine but A/C still in control.

P/O Hodgson attacked Me 110, fired long burst from beam to line astern. E/A dived out of sight with both engines stopped and white glycol smoke pouring out from underneath him. He repeated this dose on another Me 110 with exactly the same result, 5 miles E of Ramsgate. He then attacked another Me 110. Fired burst into belly of E/A from 100 yds closing to 50 yds and E/A rolled over with smoke pouring from underneath. He went along down in a controlled glide but P/O Hodgson had to break off combat due to lack of ammunition and being chased by 7 Me 110's. Previous to these encounters he damaged a Heinkel 111 during a head-on attack.

Sgt. Goodman fired long burst into Me 110 which was forced

to break formation and when last seen had port engine on fire and was losing height out to sea.

He then attacked another Me 110 from astern, set it on fire and saw it pancake on sea 4 to 5 miles S of Sandgate.

P/O Allard destroyed two He 111, the first one had both engines set on fire and was seen to crash on land by P/O English. The second one he attacked from above and beam and E/A burst into flames and dived straight down. It was believed to have crashed in field about 30 miles S.W. of Croydon.

P/O English damaged one He 111 and destroyed one Me 110 which was last seen diving steeply crab-fashion with both engines on fire.

F/O Gowers fired two bursts of five seconds into Me 110 from astern and white smoke was seen coming from both engines. E/A was followed down to within 2,000 feet of sea. He was diving slowly with one engine out of action, used no evasive tactics or answering fire and probably crashed fifteen miles out to sea off Dungeness.

F/O Woods-Scawn fired several bursts into Me 110 stopping starboard engine and setting port engine on fire. E/A dived steeply into cloud and was lost sight of, but columns of smoke seen on ground shortly afterwards. This was near Dover.

Sgt. Booth attacked and damaged one Me 110. P/O Marshall was badly shot up and obliged to bale out. He landed safely near Ashford.

Ten Hurricanes landed Croydon between 1133 and 1201 hours.

Enemy casualties; 6 Me 110 destroyed
2 He 111 destroyed
2 Me 110 probable
2 Me 110 damaged
2 He 111 damaged

Our losses: 1 Hurricane destroyed, pilot unhurt.

When we consider the losses on both sides for August 30 —thirty-six for the Germans, twenty-six for the British—it is well to remember that at the time each side had an inflated idea of the other's losses. For the Germans to exaggerate when they held all the cards, when, in fact, they were close to victory, was folly. As we shall see, it led them to even greater follies.

For the moment, however, the Luftwaffe was doing well. August 31 was featured by more attacks on the sector stations that controlled the defense of London. Croydon, Hornchurch and Debden were all bombed in the morning, Biggin Hill and Hornchurch caught it in the afternoon. This success was scored despite precautions by Fighter Command and Group Headquarters. The Operations Building at Biggin Hill was set afire and communications cut. Hurricanes of 111 Squadron by sailing into strong German force headed for Duxford broke up another German attack. But the German blows at Fighter Command's nerve centers were telling. Two of the three squadrons controlled by Biggin Hill had to be withdrawn from that station and placed under the control of others.

The pilots of Fighter Command were not rattled but they were, they said, "damned annoyed." The Hurricanes of 85 Squadron had just left the ground at Croydon when the bombs began to burst, tossing the fighters like leaves. In a brisk engagement in which Peter Townsend was wounded the squadron destroyed two Me 109's and one Me 110 but lost two of its own planes. At Hornchurch three Spitfires of 54 Squadron were destroyed as they took off, yet all three pilots survived.

Here is the record of that day's operations by 85 Squadron; its most active day during the battle.

Croydon 31/8/40—Twelve Hurricanes took off 12:25 hours to intercept E/A approaching the aerodrome. Bombs started to fall on East side of aerodrome just as aircraft were airborne.

P/O Hemingway fired a burst into a Me 109 and saw much smoke issuing from E/A.

P/O Worrall reported that before bailing out a cannon shell hit his A/C behind the cockpit and did not get through the armour plate.

S/L Townsend reported that Jaguars circled when threatened by attack although withdrawing SE.

Me 109's protected Jaguars very closely.

10 Hurricanes landed Croydon between 1340 and 1400 hours.

Enemy casualties: 2 Me 109 destroyed
1 Me 110 destroyed
1 Me 109 probable
1 Do 215 probable
2 Me 109 damaged

Our losses: 2 Hurricanes S/L Townsend wounded. P/O Worrall slightly wounded.

Croydon 31/8/40—Ten Hurricanes took off for Hawkinge at 1730 hours to patrol forward base and were then ordered to intercept E/A making for Thames estuary. About thirty Do 215's were sighted at 17:40 hours flying at 16,000 feet to 17,000 feet accompanied by approximately 100 mixed Me 109's and Me 110's and attack was opened about twenty miles S of Purfleet. The Squadron effectively broke up enemy formations and separated bombers from fighters by diving in sections in line astern in the box.

P/O Hodgson did a head-on attack on a Do 215 and saw pieces fall off nose and starboard wing. Then engaged Me 109 with a long burst, followed by a short burst at 200 yards and E/A rolled over and went down with engine on fire near Thameshaven oil storage tanks.

At this juncture P/O Hodgson's machine was hit by cannon shell which blew up his oil lines and glycol tank and set fire to his engine. He prepared to bale out and was actually half out of his aircraft when he realised that he was over a thickly populated area and also still near the oil tanks. Fully appreciating the danger he decided to remain with his aircraft and endeavour to force-land, and thus avoid the serious consequences of a flaming Hurricane crashing in the area mentioned.

By skilful sideslipping, he managed to keep the fire under control and finally succeeded in making a wheels-up landing in a field near Shotgate, Essex, narrowly missing wires and other obstacles erected with a view to preventing the landing of hostile aircraft.

P/O Marshall attacked No. 3 of leading section of bombers and gave it a five seconds burst. All bullets entered E/A and it was seen to lurch violently and dip out of formation. Before being able to verify result of attack P/O Marshall was hit in the rudder and had to break away downwards.

F/O Woods-Scawn gave a five second burst into Me 109 from dead astern and it pulled up and then spun out of sight. He then did a quarter attack on another Me 109, followed with a long burst from dead astern and E/A caught on fire and dived down with a trail of black smoke pouring from it.

P/O Allard on opening quarter attack from the sun saw a Do 215 wheel over and go down out of sight. He then attacked another Do 215 and from 200 yards closed until he nearly hit E/A. Pieces of metal flew off and one engine burst into flames as E/A went down.

Sgt Goodman fired long burst into Do 215 and saw tracers entering centre of fuselage. Had to break off combat as an Me

109 was on his tail but definitely damaged E/A as his windscreen was covered with oil from the Dornier.

Sgt. Booth attacked Me 110 from astern and fired long burst. E/A dived for about 5,000 feet and then continued to dive inverted. Sgt. Booth followed it to this point but broke away then as his A.S.I. (air speed indicator) showed 400 M.P.H. and the fabric seams on the wings were coming apart. Position a few miles W of Sittingbourne.

Sgt. Evans during head-on attack on Do 215 put port engine of E/A on fire, but was unable to see further result.

Eight Hurricanes landed Croydon 18:15 to 18:55 hours. One aircraft having refuelled at Hawkinge returned Croydon 20:10 hours.

Enemy casualties: 3 Me 109 destroyed
3 Do 215 probable
1 Me 110 probable
2 Do 215 damaged

Our losses: 1 Hurricane damaged (force-landed)

Nine Hurricanes took off Croydon 19:17 hours to patrol Hawkinge and then were ordered to intercept Raid 18c. The first indication of position of E/A was given by AA fire from Dover and then nine Me 109 were seen flying at about 15,000 feet. The Squadron circled out to sea as E/A on left, then wheeled in and caught them by surprise when individual combats ensued.

P/O Allard opened fire on E/A from 150 yards astern and parts of the wing appeared to break off. E/A dived down and crashed near Folkestone either on land or just in the sea.

F/O Woods-Scawn carried out beam attack causing E/A to dive steeply, then gave a further burst from astern and E/A went down on fire with wing tank burning—confirmed by P/O Lewis.

P/O Lewis fired a four seconds burst at E/A from 150 yards

on the beam and from slightly below. Black smoke billowed out and E/A dived steeply. P/O Lewis followed it down to 5,000 feet making sure it was done for and rejoined squadron. Position then above sea near Folkestone.

F/O Gowers fired two bursts of five seconds and seven seconds, caused a large piece to blow out of port wing of E/A. Petrol streamed out as E/A dived vertically and when Gowers left him at 4,000 feet he was still diving straight down and by then was in flames. Confirmed by P/O Lewis.

Nine Hurricanes landed Croydon 2005 hours to 2022 hours.
Enemy casualties: 4 Me 109 destroyed
Our losses: Nil.

So August ended for the squadron. It had been a month of harsh, ceaseless activity, valiant and successful fighting, during which the pilots flew 1,019 hours and 50 minutes, a record for No. 85. Of this 853 and one-half hours was operational flying. In those hours the squadron believed it had destroyed forty-four German aircraft, twenty-two of them Me 109's, probably destroyed fifteen more and damaged fifteen other German planes. Flight Lieutenants H. R. Hamilton and Dickie Lee were lost. Peter Townsend was wounded and three other pilots slightly wounded. Eight of the squadron's Hurricanes had been destroyed, three others were damaged. The faces, young and unlined a few months before, were lined and infinitely weary now. There was less kidding and horseplay in the squadron. They were fighting for their lives and a good deal more.

On August 31 the Germans lost forty-one planes, the RAF thirty-nine. This was not the sort of loss ratio Dowding wanted during September.

That month opened with the Germans still punishing the sector stations. Biggin Hill was damaged so badly by a major raid on September 1 that equipment had to be moved out of the unsafe buildings into the open. There were the men and women who ran the station, the people with that cold, two-o'clock in the morning bravery that is so important and so much less appreciated than the bravery of open fight, went about their business. Sometimes the girls cried when they heard of the death of a man up there above. Once a ground officer apologized to them for the language of the pilots. The girls were indignant. They understood. They recognized the nervous need for sudden gusts of profanity. They knew what the battle was about.

Back came the Germans. Hornchurch, North Weald, West Malling and other, less important fields were all bombed once or more during the next few days. The damage was greatest at North Weald, where the telephone wires were severed and hangars set on fire. Fighter Command had ordered the squadrons to hunt in pairs whenever possible. This tactic did not help much against the massed formations of German bombers safe in their cocoon of fighters.

The British were still shooting down more German planes than they themselves lost. But the margin was not a big one and some days the ratio went the other way. September 1, fifteen British to fourteen German; September 2, thirty-one to thirty-five; September 3, sixteen and sixteen; September 4, seventeen and twenty-five; September 5, twenty and twenty-three; September 6, twenty-three and thirty-five.

Between August 29 and September 7 there were thirty-three major German attacks, twenty-three of them on airfields. Air Vice-Marshal Park reported that "the enemy's bombing attacks by day did extensive damage to five of our forward aerodromes and also to six of our seven sector stations. By September 5 the damage was having a serious effect on fighting efficiency. The absence of many telephone lines, the use of scratch equipment in emergency operations rooms and the general dislocation of ground organisation was seriously felt in the handling of squadrons."

Many experienced officers surveying the damage done to the airfields wondered if the Germans would not follow up these attacks with parachutists. Determined men supplied by air might have held the airdromes and won a foothold for other, heavier reinforcements. There was no shortage in the German army of determined, efficient soldiers or commanders. But the airborne forces remained out of the battle.

All British losses in those days were heavy losses. The repair and maintenance squadrons did their best. But on September 6 the number of additional Spitfires and Hurricanes ready for use stood at 125.

The transfer of pilots from the Bomber and Coastal Commands and the Royal Navy's Fleet Air Arm to Fighter Command after short conversion courses did not suffice. Fighter Command's strength in pilots had stood at 1,434 at the end of July. By the end of August it was 1,023.

Slowly, almost imperceptibly, the communications systems and the airfields were being battered to bits, the pilot force was bleeding to death, the reserves of aircraft were nearing the danger point. The end was not yet. But there were men who now say they could see the end in those first days of September. It was not a pretty picture.

But it was a picture seen and understood by only a very few people who understood airpower and what it could and could not do. The remainder of the country preserved its air of cheery, confident calm. The dance bands in London were reviving song hits of the recent decade. There had been few new British tunes of note and no one wanted to dance to the unhappy memories of "We're Going to Hang Out the Washing on the Siegfried Line." So the young men in uniform and their girls danced to "Where and When" and other imports from the United States. More and more people were whistling an English tune, "A Nightingale Sang in Berkeley Square," of which the Fighter Command pilots thought highly. Quentin Reynolds, reporting with sympathy and courage the British resistance, had written a bawdy additional lyric to the tune whose last line was "There were six miscarriages under Claridge's when a screaming bomb fell in Berkeley Square." The letter columns of the *Times* reflected a brisk debate on whether racing should be resumed. On the morning of August 30, when the Luftwaffe was gathering its strength for the onslaught upon the sector stations, the editor was informed: "Surely this is a very rare, if not a unique occurrence. For three years in succession a pair of wagtails have built their nest over our front door among the creepers."

The course of any great battle is influenced by actions and reactions far from the field of the battle itself. This was true of the Battle of Britain. The reactions were largely German; the actions British. The Germans were deluded. The British benefited from that curious tendency of the Germans in war to misinterpret and misuse success. They did it in 1914 on the Marne. They were now to do it again in 1940 over Britain.

To understand what happened we must remember that to the Germans the air offensive on Britain was the essential preliminary to invasion. If the RAF was driven from the skies, then the invasion could proceed with a very good chance of success. While the Luftwaffe had been fighting the British, the preparations for the invasion had gone forward. By the beginning of September the German Naval Staff had collected—by requisition—168 transports of over 700,000 tons, 1,910 barges, 419 tugs and trawlers, and about 1,600 motorboats. These craft had moved along the rivers and canals of Western Europe to the ports of North Germany, France and the Low Countries, where they presented a tempting target. On September 6, for instance, British photographic reconnaissance brought back the news that 205 barges lay in the port of Ostend. The British reasoned that the sea transport would not be concentrated in ports within easy range of Bomber Command unless invasion was imminent.

Consequently, on the night of September 6 Blenheim

medium bombers began a series of attacks on the concentrations of shipping in the Channel ports. The next night the Blenheims were joined by Hampden and Battle bombers. In the offensive they dropped more than 1,000 tons of bombs; in those days and for those aircraft a respectable total. Nevertheless, the Germans doggedly continued their preparations and the official historian's assessment is that by September 15, a critical date in every respect, "the enemy's dispositions for the invasion of this country were either complete or on the threshold of completion." On the British side the Joint Intelligence Committee on September 7 informed the Chiefs of Staff that invasion might be imminent.

The British bombing attacks on the invasion ports and other relatively light raids upon communications and industrial plants in Germany had two reactions on the would-be invaders. As we know, the army and navy high commands had been given an inflated idea of the Luftwaffe's success against the RAF. The Germans guessed that Bomber Command had lost some of its pilots to Fighter Command. They had been told of extensive damage to its airfields. Yet here were the British bombers returning night after night. The raids might not be especially heavy or particularly effective, but the bombers were there, ready for action. What would they do to the masses of transports and barges when, loaded with troops, they attempted to cross the Channel on the invasion? And the British fleet, was it not still in being wrapped in the northern mists? No, neither the generals nor the admirals liked the look of things. There was something odd about the Luftwaffe's claims. Goering must do better if they were to take the risk.

Enter now Hitler, breathing fire and smoke. On the night of August 24–25 a few German bombs had fallen, probably unintentionally, upon the center of London. Bomber Command, on the Prime Minister's order, retaliated with a raid on Berlin. It was a small affair compared with the great raids of 1943, 1944 and 1945 but Hitler was very angry indeed.

"If they attack our cities, we will rub out their cities from the map," he shouted. "The hour will come when one of us two will break and it will not be Nazi Germany." Fine bloodcurdling stuff, although no one in Britain appeared particularly impressed. Goering, the one Nazi leader who, as an experienced airman, might have been expected to take a realistic view of the air battle, followed the leader. It may be that the Reichsmarschall was mesmerized by the exaggerated figures of British losses fed him by the Luftwaffe. At any rate he was prepared to switch the attack from the airfields and sector stations to London.

Goering certainly did not lack expert advice to the contrary. He called a conference at The Hague on September 3 with Sperrle and Kesselring, the commanders of Luftflotten III and II, respectively, and the usual staff officers, intelligence experts and sycophants in attendance. Sperrle spoke up arguing for the continuation of the attacks on the airfields. He insisted that Fighter Command still had about a thousand fighters left and that it would be unwise to discontinue the attacks on their bases until there was a more appreciable slackening of British resistance in the air. Kesselring, an invincible optimist then and later in the war, took a contrary view. The British, he proclaimed, "have next to nothing left." Only bad weather, he said, had prevented his bombers from reaching all their targets. Finally Colonel Joseph Schmid, chief of Luftwaffe intelligence, declared flatly that the British had no more than 350 fighters remaining. He erred by 300; Fighter Command at that date had about 650 aircraft in the squadrons ready for action.

Schmid's mistaken estimate emboldened Goering. He told his generals that the British had only saved their fighter force by pulling the squadrons back from the forward airfields. An offensive against London, he predicted, would force the RAF to use its final reserves of Spitfires and Hurricanes. The decision was taken. London was to be the next target and it was to begin on September 7.

This was one of the gravest tactical mistakes on the German side in the whole battle. In fact, since the outcome of the Battle of Britain had such great influence on the subsequent course of the war, it must be accounted one of the signal German errors of World War II. Why was it made?

Faulty intelligence certainly played a large part. We have noted Schmid's erroneous estimate of British fighter strength. This, of course, was attributable to the exaggerated estimates of British losses in the Luftwaffe. But all through this period, almost from the end of Dunkirk until the end of the Battle of Britain, the German services generally were ill-served by their intelligence branches. The estimates of the strength of the British army in Britain in July, for instance, were ridiculously exaggerated. Then and later in the war the Germans showed a tendency to underrate the British when they were opposing them in the field and to overrate them, especially in numbers, at other times. Reading the accounts on both sides of the hill, one is forced repeatedly to conclude that the desire to tell the Fuehrer and his entourage what they wanted to hear, the interservice bickerings that in this case led the Luftwaffe to play down its own reverses and exaggerate those of the British, and the heady effects of a series of unprecedented victories on the Continent all blinded the Germans to the real situation.

Folly bred more folly. The Germans entered the offensive against London convinced that prolonged bombing would break the will of the people of the city, drive the government from the capital, and at the same time force Fighter Command to actions it could not win and which, in the end, would eliminate it as a factor in the defense of Britain.

Whatever the causes of this monumental error, the fact is that the German High Command ignored one of the first rules of war by turning the attack from an air force that was still fighting hard but had been very badly mauled and much weakened to the vast forest of brick and concrete of London. Another week's hard hammering at the airfields and sector stations could have meant disaster for the British. When the pressure had been lifted from these targets, Air Vice-Marshal Park wrote: "Had the enemy continued his heavy attacks against Biggin Hill and the adjacent sectors and knocked out their operations rooms or telephone communications, the fighter defences of London would have been in a perilous state during the last critical phase when heavy attacks have been directed against the capital."

Through the first six days of September the war gradually crept closer to London. On the 1st some bombers attacked the docks at Tilbury. On the 3rd, when the British editorial writers were reviewing the course of the first year of the war with what seems today to be an almost unbelievable complacency, factories in the Medway towns and at Weybridge were bombed. Finally, on the eve of the major assault, Luftwaffe formations penetrated to Thameshaven and bombed the oil-storage facilities there with considerable success.

That was a long, golden summer and the first week of September was no exception. My memory is of bright suns and clear blue skies. London was gay; so unused to air raids that when the sirens sounded people went to the rooftops to watch the fun. In Whitehall officials talked of the coming presidential election—"Who is this fellow Willkie?"—as if the war still was something far away and slightly unreal. If ordinary folk discussed it, they used sporting terms: "I hear we were eighty-four for fifteen," they said, meaning eighty-four Germans planes had been shot down for the loss of fifteen British. They were in good heart. They would need to be.

Chapter VIII

*. . . we would rather see London laid in ruin
and ashes than that it should be tamely and ab-
jectly enslaved.*

—WINSTON CHURCHILL in a radio broadcast

We now approach the climax of the German effort in the
West in 1940. Never again were they so close to victory.
Never again was the cause of liberty in such danger. To
this point our narrative has been chiefly concerned with
the contending air forces. Now the picture broadens. We
must watch the great trial of strength that pitted German
bombs, and the fatigue, destruction and temporary chaos
that they brought, against the resolution of the people of
London. Beyond the Channel and the massed German
divisions we must watch the effect of what happened in
and over London upon the German High Command and
that group of very able men, buffoons and lightweights
who made up Hitler's curious court.

The basic military concept behind the attack on London,
as we have seen, was that it would force the weakened
RAF to battle. This battle, the Germans were convinced,
would end in the elimination of Fighter Command and
Operation "Sea Lion" could begin. But there was a second
concept strongly supported by some of the politico-military figures on the highest level of the Nazi party. This

was that a great air offensive against London would sap the will to resist of the British people and induce them to surrender. As we now know, this was another German underestimate of British psychology. It was also a gross exaggeration of the effect of air bombardment on an enormous capital peopled by men and women who not only were brave and resolute but who enjoyed a great capacity for improvisation and a high degree of mechanical and technical skill.

The daylight attacks—the German plan for bombing London envisaged raids by day and by night—were to be made on the same basis as those that had done so much damage to Fighter Command in the second phase of the battle. The bombers were to be heavily protected by fighter escort and no attack was to be made unless such escort in strength was available.

The offensive against London did not catch the British totally unawares. They had been alerted to a change in German tactics by the bombing in the Medway and at Thameshaven, near to London. Dowding and Park both realized that London's sprawling dockland along the Thames, the great London railway termini, and the aircraft factories scattered south and southwest of London were inviting targets to the Germans.

The British had a great deal to do and very little time and straitened resources to do it with. First the RAF's communications network, badly disrupted by the attacks on the sector stations, had to be restored. Royal Engineers and men of the Post Office were called in to help in this work and to establish alternative systems should the stations be subjected to further destructive attacks. For the British could only guess that the attack would be switched to London. Knowing their own weakness and ignorant of the German errors of judgment, they feared that, after all, the Luftwaffe might resume the attacks on the airfields and communications.

Fighter Command thus assumed a double task. First, it would have to cover the targets, especially aircraft factories, in and around London. Second, it would have to continue the defense of the sector stations. To assure the maximum defensive strength Park asked for help from No. 10 Group to the west and No. 12 Group north of the Thames. The former was to intervene if German bombers appeared in the Brooklands area while the latter was to assist No. 11 Group should the Luftwaffe strike at the airfields north and northeast of London.

Special tactical instructions also were issued to No. 11 Group. Park believed that his squadrons, in their natural desire to get above the Germans before launching their attacks, had been flying too high and attacking too late. He wanted the fighters to let the German fighters alone and attack the bombers. Some of the Spitfires could engage the German fighters but the bulk of the British defense force in any engagement was to concentrate on the bombers. His instructions said that "whenever time permits squadrons are to be put into battle in pairs. The enemy's main attack must be met with maximum strength between the coast and our line of sector stations."

See p. 91,
lines 1-2:
they can't
both be right!

September 7 was a Saturday. Across the Atlantic the beaches and resorts were crowded. The politicians' voices were loud in the land. America was to be saved by helping the Allies, which at that time meant Britain, or America was to be saved by staying completely out of things. A family in New York wrote to a relative in London that the fighting seemed very confused. No one seemed to know who was winning or losing. But there were other distractions. The New York Yankees, oddly enough, were not going to win the pennant that year and the football season was not far off.

Londoners took advantage of another wonderful day. But the days were growing shorter and there were signs that this winter would be different. *The Westerner* and *When the Daltons Rode* were showing at West End movie houses and audiences were surprised to see bomber pilots on leave admiring the gunplay. There were few unwounded fighter pilots about.

The German attack began late that afternoon. Goering, who now assumed command and personal direction of the offensive, sent the largest formation available compatible with the principle of adequate fighter cover for the bombers: 372 bombers and 642 fighters. The force's targets were the docks and oil installations along the Thames.

Despite all the preparations by the defenders, the German force had pushed well past the coast before contact was made. Fighter Command's sensitivity over the sector stations tied a number of squadrons to the protection of these targets. The German force, of course, naturally did not fly as a single formation but in well-organized groups, each of which forced its way through the very heavy anti-aircraft fire toward the docks. The first targets to be bombed were the Royal Arsenal at Woolwich and two factories nearby. These attacks took place at about 5:15 P.M. The Germans had drawn first blood and had done it without being seriously engaged except by the antiaircraft batteries.

This did not last long. The British put twenty-three squadrons into the air that day and twenty-one of them engaged the Germans. The force that had bombed Woolwich drew off to the north and then swung east. It was engaged by no less than seven squadrons. The antiaircraft fire had already broken up the bomber formation and the Spitfires and Hurricanes, picking individual aircraft as their prey, did a good deal of damage. But their concentration on this force cost the British dear elsewhere. Two other German formations bombed the docks at West Ham and Thameshaven without being intercepted.

Still the German planes came out of the east. There could be no doubt now that London was the target. One formation was jumped by four British squadrons as it flew at what seemed like a leisurely pace over the Thames. The scene lives still in my memory.

From somewhere on the left, probably from the burning warehouses near Commercial Docks, a great cylinder of black smoke climbed steadily contrasting with fat, fleecy clouds in the distance. The streets of the City of London below me were clamorous with the noise of fire engines and the shouts of running men. Looking down toward Ludgate Circus I saw a policeman running in the direction of the fire. Until then all London policemen had appeared as massive men of magisterial calm standing aloof, untouched by events around them. This fellow was pelting across Ludgate Circus toward St. Paul's. But somehow the noise on the streets seemed inconsequential. For just to the right of that great cylinder of smoke and slightly above it were the German planes. The sun, already sinking, caught them as they turned. The puffs of antiaircraft bursts that had blossomed below them suddenly stopped. Another plane, smaller than the bombers, had darted into the formation from above. Then another. The clamor of the streets was all around us but there was no sound from that battle in the sky. One of the bombers abruptly changed course and fell off to the south. Now there were other British planes in the melee. So this was a dog fight. My hands shook in excitement. The breeze brought a whiff of smoke.

The dog fight I watched that day was one of the few in which the British fighters broke up and dispersed a German formation before it could do much damage. But many other Germans broke through. Docks and warehouses had been set alight and the people of London's East End suffered heavy casualties when strings of bombs fell in the neighborhoods near the docks. The Germans had dropped over 300 tons of high explosive bombs and many thousands of incendiaries. London's long agony had begun.

That day the Germans lost forty-one aircraft. But again

the British lost heavily and again they could afford it less. Twenty-eight fighters were shot down, sixteen were badly damaged, and seventeen pilots were killed or badly wounded. And despite this sacrifice the Germans had done great damage.

The success of the German daylight attack was not the sole reason for British concern. For some days past the British Chiefs of Staff had been studying the German position. They knew from photographic reconnaissance of the concentration of shipping and other invasion preparations along the French, Belgian and Dutch coasts. Four German spies who had been captured had disclosed that their mission was to inform the German High Command of the movement of troop reinforcements to the invasion area. The attack on London, the center of England's communications and the seat of government, strengthened the impression that the greatest challenge of all was upon the islanders. At 8:00 P.M., therefore, General Headquarters of Home Forces sent the code word "Cromwell" to the army's Southern and Eastern Commands. "Cromwell" meant "Invasion imminent."

So that night the army stood to its weapons, pitifully few in number still but many more than they had been two months before. The Home Guard, some with shotguns, some with rifles sent from the United States, and some with only revolvers and a few rounds of ammunition took up their positions. In some areas the church bells were rung denoting the actual start of invasion. Spinsters in country villages saw parachutes dangling against the starlight. Men with strange accents were liable to be summarily challenged in remote regions. Along the coasts men peered into the Channel mists expecting to see a German armada materialize. But the only action the army saw that night was in the antiaircraft batteries.

For the Germans returned. The day raid had left huge fires burning at half a dozen places along the river. Now in the darkness the first of over 250 bombers began to thread their way toward the capital. What some called the Battle of London and what the Londoners themselves called "the Blitz" had begun.

I dined that night, very tired and shaken, with a colonel of the United States Army Air Force whom I had met shortly before. His name was Carl A. Spaatz and he had been in London for some weeks watching the battle. We dined at Rule's and midway through the meal we heard the high, keening scream of a bomber in a shallow dive. Paddy, the waiter, volunteered that the Germans were "at it again."

"By God," Spaatz said, "that's good, that's fine. The British are winning." I remarked that it hadn't looked like it that afternoon. "Of course they're winning," he said vehemently. "The Germans can't bomb at night—hell, I don't think they're very good in daylight—but they haven't been trained for night bombing. Nope, the British have got them now. They've forced them to bomb at night. The Krauts must be losing more than we know."

I suggested that night bombing in the end might succeed in beating the British to their knees.

"Not in a million years," Spaatz said. "I tell you the Germans don't know how to go about it. And look at this bunch here. Do they look worried or scared? We're both a damned sight scareder than they are. The Germans won't beat them that way. Nope, the Germans have been licked in daylight."

Four years later when he was General Spaatz, commanding the United States Eighth Air Force and a mighty figure, I reminded him of the conversation. "Goes to show you that colonels are mighty smart fellows—sometimes," he said.

The British had been fairly well prepared for the start of the bombing offensive by daylight. They were less well prepared in the opening rounds of the night battle.

The principal British weapon against raiders by night was the antiaircraft gun. Theoretically about thirty single-engined fighters drawn from No. 11 Group also were available. But unless visibility was close to perfect these had little chance of seeing and engaging a German bomber except through sheer good luck. Radar, which later led to an increasingly high total of "kills" by night, was not introduced to squadrons until that winter and, when it was, twin-engined fighters were used. The one squadron of Blenheims then available lacked radar sets and operators. So all depended on the guns.

There were not enough of them. Before the war the Committee of Imperial Defence had decided that 480 heavy antiaircraft guns were required for the defense of London. On September 7 there were 264 available and the men serving many of these had been in action that day. Only ninety-two of the total were deployed in what was called the "inner artillery zone." The batteries relied on sound locators, which soon proved ineffective. That night the first bombs fell on Battersea soon after 8:30. The guns of the inner defenses did not open fire until nine o'clock. Thereafter for nearly seven hours the Germans flew at will over the great mass of London guided by the fires lit that afternoon and by others started by night. All told they used over 250 bombers without losing a single one to British action. The guns pounded away. The searchlights probed the skies. A Blenheim and a Beaufighter, a new twin-engined fighter, equipped with experimental radar sets were on patrol but failed to engage a single German plane. All night long they droned in over the Thames and over Portsmouth and Southampton and in the fields and on the downs the British stood to arms. That was the military side of the opening of the Blitz.

Throughout the period after Dunkirk the British were like gamblers who had entered a poker game with scanty resources. In the air battles by day they had bet that the superior skill of their pilots plus the eight-gun fighter plus the radar network and the communications system would defeat superior numbers of Germans. In the first weeks of the bombing of London they held poorer cards. Prime Minister Churchill and his Cabinet bet that the courage and resolution of the Londoners, on which they counted but about which they as yet knew very little, and the vast expanse of the city itself would enable London to survive the ordeal of continued bombing. They knew that London's defenses were deficient in antiaircraft guns. They also knew that, even if they had all the guns called for by prewar estimates, these guns would not be enough to halt or even to slow down the German offensive by night. For the rudimentary means of tracking enemy aircraft then used by the antiaircraft command were not accurate enough to ensure sufficient hits to make the Germans pause.

From the night of September 7 to November 3 an average of 250 German bombers attacked London every night. There were many heavier attacks during the war; London endured nothing like the weight of bombs that fell on Berlin. But no attack was as prolonged. This was the first and most important phase of the Battle of London that was to continue sporadically for another four and one-half years until the last German V-2 rocket base was captured by the advancing armies of the Allies. It was the most important phase because so much rested upon the outcome. Had the people of London broken under the assault, the prospects for British survival as a fighting power in the war would have been very dim.

The first massive night raid was an accurate foretaste of what was to come. The Germans dropped about 330 tons of high explosive and over 1,000 incendiaries. Almost the entire load fell within a ten-mile radius of Charing Cross. The worst-damaged area was along the river east of the City of London, where the fires lit by the bombers that afternoon guided the German planes. The huge power station at Battersea was hit. So was a smaller one at West Ham. Three railroad lines out of the capital were closed for brief periods and a score of new fires were lit.

During the raids on September 7 by day and night about 1,000 Londoners were killed. To put these civilian casualties in proportion it should be noted that after D day, 1944, the United States First Army reported 1,465 killed in action.

The British communiqué said: "Fires were caused among industrial targets. Damage was done to lighting and other public services, and some dislocation to communications was caused. Attacks have also been directed against the docks. Information as to casualties is not yet available."

In these terms the raid was nothing, an incident in a vast conflict. In human terms it was a terrifying ordeal for those on whom the bombs fell and an awakening for those who had nursed the secret conviction that, come what may, the war would not touch them. That evening, when the sun had set, watchers in the West End of London saw a sight that was to become shockingly familiar: the dome of St. Paul's silhouetted against the orange glow of the fires burning in the City and the East End. Fire itself was an enemy, more tangible, quite as ruthless, and less predictable than the Germans. By midnight there were nine great fires raging in London. One of these, in the Quebec Yard, Surrey Docks, was the biggest fire London had known in this century. The firemen, both the regulars of the London Fire Department and the amateurs of the

Auxiliary Fire Service, had seen nothing like this. The heat was so great that it blistered the paint on fireboats on the far bank of the Thames and set alight the wooden paving blocks. Flaming bits of wood six or seven inches long were thrown off by the roaring holocaust to start other fires. In the warehouses stores of rum, paint, sugar and wheat caught fire. Barrels of rum exploded and the burning liquor cascaded out of the buildings. The firemen worked literally until they dropped from the heat or from exhaustion. Yet to the men of the AFS, after the first wondering fear, there came a strange sort of exhilaration. One of them told me that he had had enough during the preceding winter of sharp comments about wasting his time as a fireman. There was real work to be done in other services, he was told. Now on that terrible night he and his mates were needed.

Bermondsey, Poplar, Woolwich and West Ham were the centers of destruction. On that first night, oddly enough, there were more signs of panic than there were later in the Blitz. People were unnerved by the suddenness and fearfulness of the destruction. Men and women wanted to get out, to the country, to the West End, anywhere away from the bombs. They thought their shelters inadequate in numbers and in strength, which was largely true, they found the local authorities disorganized, as indeed they were, especially in West Ham. They knew that the bombers would come again and again, as they did.

That night Goering informed the people of Germany: "This is the historic hour, when for the first time our air force delivered its thrust right into the enemy's heart."

This is not a history of the Blitz. Those who want one should read Constantine Fitz Gibbon's *The Blitz*, the best and most moving record I know of those terrible hours. But any assessment of the air war of 1940 must take into account what the Germans did and did not do in those first night raids. We are accustomed to German exaggeration about the Battle of Britain. In describing what they had done in the Battle of London, the propagandists severed all connection with the truth.

It was said, for instance, that the raids had eliminated London as a seaport. This was untrue. The bombers had done a great amount of damage to warehouses and homes near the docks. But a dock itself is a difficult target to knock out. The Port of London continued to play its part in the economy although inevitably it suffered from a shortage of dock workers. Woolwich, site of an arsenal and several important factories, suffered considerably during the early raids. Yet it was not knocked out of the war, as the Germans claimed. A vast amount of stored commodities, important to a nation living on perilously thin lifelines stretching out from the island to the world, were destroyed. Railroad communications were damaged that first night and damaged again and again during the later bombings. But the railroads kept going, performing prodigies then and later in the war.

London was so vast that the Germans with the bombers and bombs available to them in 1940 could not inflict the punishment on the city that their propagandists imagined. When, later in the Blitz, the antiaircraft batteries were reinforced in numbers—although their firing remained inaccurate—the German pilots were deterred from seeking out and bombing accurately those targets whose destruction might have crippled London's usefulness as an armory, a citadel and a communications center.

No one who endured the Blitz and who thinks back to those days can escape a feeling of wonderment. Wonderment that people whom life had given so little, people who, it might be thought, could not conceivably be worse off under any form of government, should show such courage and resolution in the face of the nightly terror and destruction from the skies. For the first attacks by night, as well as by day, fell on the poorest section of London; the huddled masses living in squalid tenements and decaying rows of brick houses near the docks. In the preceding decade these people had known long stretches of unemployment and the deadening effect of the dole. They had seen the country "fit for heroes to live in" turned into a country fit for the rich and the middle class to live in. Their own political hopes had been shattered by Ramsay MacDonald's betrayal of the Labour party. Bemused by pornographic newspapers, befuddled by beer, deprived, save in very rare cases, of the opportunity to rise from their sordid surroundings, they formed the base, the unknown, unknowing base of British society.

Now night after night the bombs clawed the guts out of their pathetic lives. Their few possessions—the pieces of furniture so carefully guarded in the front parlor, the hideous bits of pottery stamped "A Present from South-end," the fading photographs of Uncle Syd in his uniform before he went to France in 1914—were torn from their familiar surroundings and scattered in the streets. The poor, mean houses were shattered and burned. One evening they were there. In the morning there was nothing, nothing. Streets counted their dead not in ones and twos but in tens and twenties. There was no rest; and, as the raids continued, precious little hope.

The boast "London can take it" was trumpeted around the world. Indeed London could. But there was a great difference in the ways of taking the medicine Goering's bombers spooned out night after night. It was tedious and difficult but not especially rigorous to "take it," if the phrase meant going to bed in a deep shelter beneath an apartment house after a good dinner and a few drinks. But for the mass of the people of London who endured those first strokes of the German lash "taking it" meant something far different. They slept in flimsy surface shelters, in movie houses, in the crypts of churches or beneath old warehouses. For them there was no prospect of a weekend in the country or even a night in the country. They had to stay.

Courage was not the special province of the poor. A great many upper-class Londoners treated the German bombing with a sort of grim contempt. They were not going to be driven from their beds or from familiar house-hold habits by Hitler. When "it," meaning the bombing,

seemed too close, they donned dressing gowns and went to
the kitchen for the inevitable cup of tea. I heard a man
say, "If I'm going to die, I'm going to die in my own house.
No shelter for me."

He had a good deal of company. The statisticians estimated that sixty-four out of every hundred Londoners
stayed in their own beds, moving out of them to the shelter of the stairs only when the bombs seemed uncomfortably near. For the rest nine of each hundred slept in the
public shelters and twenty-seven in their own Anderson
shelters provided by the government. The poor of the East
End fled to the public shelters. It was in these shelters
that the spirit of resistance was slowly born. It did not
emerge suddenly. The romantic theory that London's initial response was one of defiance is an exaggeration.

The shelter I remember best was in Spitalfields. I went
there one Friday night. I stood at the top of a long flight
of stairs. Outside the bombers were droning overhead. In
a cone of dim light at the foot of the stairs stood a tiny
figure. Then a voice, a man's voice, called "Come on down
and have a cuppa." His name was Micky Brown. He was
about four feet tall. But when you knew him you never
noticed his lack of height. He was an optician, but his tiny
shop had been destroyed in one of the early raids. Here
in the shelter he was the boss. He had made himself the
boss by sheer personality and organizing ability.

The people of the shelter had been divided by Micky
into three groups: families, single men, and single women.
Partitions, flimsy and not very high, provided what privacy

was possible. The "rooms" were decorated: old photographs carried from home or the wreckage of home, pictures of Churchill or the King cut from the illustrated papers, a "best" teapot, a case of tarnished First War medals.

In one a woman of about forty with fine eyes and broken teeth was knitting by the light of a single electric bulb. Two girls, small and painfully thin, slept fitfully on a single cot. The woman smiled and said to Micky, "John's on duty. Is it bad?"

"Not yet, Mrs. Ford."

"'Er 'usband's a fireman," said Micky as we walked on. "It's bad 'ere for those kids. But they won't send them away. They're afraid of the country.

"We try to distribute the work fairly," Micky said. "Mrs. Ford there, she cleans up 'er own little place first and this week she's in charge of that lot that cleans the men's section. The men bring in the water in the morning before they leave. We've only got one bleedin' tap for the lot. 'Tisn't right, you know. We've got some pails, too, and some of them chemical toilets but not enough. Got a couple of doctors, assigned by the borough. Couple of others come down when they can. We can do everything but a major operation in our first-aid room. Them doctors are afraid of an epidemic. So am I, mister."

That life, as it continued, developed its own problems. The old people, especially the single men and women, didn't want to leave the shelter at any time.

"But them as has work to do," Micky said, "they go out

every morning and come back at night. The women go 'ome and cook food for the night—if there's any gas. Then they eat their tea 'ere. It's nice the way everyone tries to help everyone else."

I asked him if anyone talked about the war or giving in. He shrugged:

"Of course there's them that 'ollers about the government not doin' more for them and them what says we went into the war without arms, but they don't talk about giving up. They want to see the Germans cracked, though. Fellow came in the other night, Communist, 'e was, and wanted them all to go up to the Savoy and make a row. Laughed at 'im, they did."

Nearby was Christ Church. In the bone-deep chill of the crypt men, women and children lay on dirty quilts. Some slept in great stone coffins. The warden said they thought this protected them from blast.

A baby cried. A woman woke, comforted it, opened her dress and gave it her breast. The woman looked up: "Awful ain't it, but we can't get in to them big shelters and those ones on the street are terrible dangerous."

When I came out I saw Micky's small figure standing by the door of his shelter. There was the rumbling roar of a stick of bombs falling across the river and that never-to-be-forgotten, belly-turning rustling, crackling and cracking sound of a building crashing. "Someone's copped it," said Micky. As I left he said:

"Tell them we're not cryin' about it. It's like Churchill said, 'It's up to us.' But tell 'em it's no bloody picnic."

Another night I visited a shelter beneath a warehouse close to the river. Over two hundred people lay in groups on its cold stone floor. There had been some trouble on the first night. Lascars from the docks had raped a fourteen-year-old girl. Now the older men had formed a vigilante society. The Lascars were forbidden the place. The stink of sweat, dirty clothing, urine and excrement caught at one's nose and throat.

These were the people who saved London's name. In their humility, their cheerfulness, their stolid, unspoken determination to continue there was a splendor. It was this quiet resolution that was far more impressive than the ribald jokes about Hitler and his court, the little paper Union Jacks stuck in the heaps of rubble, the slogans "God Save the King" and "Give it to them" chalked on blackened walls. All people are brave. When their time came, the Germans endured much heavier bombing with fortitude. What distinguished the British experience was that at a time when almost every broadcast, every newspaper headline told of reverses, defeats and defections, the people of London kept their heads and their hearts intact. They could not, they would not be driven or frightened out of what they dimly comprehended they had to do. This was to fight on.

Once in the early morning I saw them coming out of the shelters; dirty, ghastly pale in the silver light of morning. The Germans were still throwing an occasional day raid at London. But back they went to the cold, dreary houses that were their homes to cook a hot breakfast and send "the old man" off to work. That morning they were extremely angry because a bobby had told them Buckingham Palace had "copped it." At the time the bombing of the palace was held by the know-it-alls at the Ministry of Information to be a welcome mistake by the Germans since it would unite crown and people, rich and poor in a feeling of sacrifice and resolution. But these people took it entirely differently. They appeared to resent the bombing of the palace as an affront; something that should not happen even in war. So they went back to their jobs.

All this lay in the future. However, the Germans had done enough on the night of September 7 to make people eye the sky anxiously in the morning. But the strain of their recent operations and bad weather conditions reduced the German attacks on September 8 to a few minor raids. September 9 saw the Luftwaffe back on the job, confident it had reached the final, victorious phase of the long battle. For the German intelligence officers had assumed, on the strength of the reports from returning pilots on the 7th, that the RAF was at last showing signs of severe strain.

There was a good deal of truth in this, although, on this point, as on others, the Germans exaggerated. During the first days of December the squadrons of Fighter Command had on the average only sixteen of their full roster of twenty-six fighter pilots. In his dispatch on the battle Dowding reported: "By the beginning of September, the incidence of casualties became so serious that a fresh squadron would become depleted and exhausted before any of the resting and re-forming squadrons was ready to take its place."

At the end of that week Dowding found he had no fresh squadrons available to relieve the battered formations in the front line. The burden still was heaviest on No. 11 Group. But both No. 10 Group to the west and No. 12 Group to the north had been heavily and continuously engaged and there was no question of using their squadrons to replace those of No. 11 Group. His solution was to divide his squadrons into categories A, B and C. The first, or A, category squadrons were to be maintained at full strength in fully trained pilots. B squadrons were to be maintained at full strength. There were to be only five of these, and it was Dowding's intention to use them only when one of the A formations had to be replaced as a unit. The C squadrons were to be allowed only a half dozen, tested veterans. Their job was to train new pilots who ultimately would move to the A and B squadrons.

During this period, incidentally, both Dowding and Park were under considerable pressure from highly placed colleagues in the RAF to make sweeping changes in their defensive arrangements. As we shall see, this pressure developed into sharp criticism that affected the whole of Fighter Command. But these difficulties came into the open after the day battle had been won. It is sufficient at this point to note that a few officers were urging Dowding to reinforce No. 11 Group. This he refused to do. He believed that extensive reinforcement would reduce the speed and efficiency with which the group could be directed and controlled in the air, offer the Germans more targets on the congested airfields, and give them an opportunity to shift their attack to other parts of Britain where fighter defense was weaker.

Although it did not seem so in those September days, the Luftwaffe was having troubles of its own. Although it still had more planes and pilots than the RAF, aircraft production in Germany was beginning to fall. British production, on the other hand, had risen from 1,279, including 325 fighters, in May to 1,601, of which 476 were fighters, in August. Tactically the Germans also felt they had not mastered the technique of fighter protection for their bombers. But as the bombers and fighters rose from the airfields east of the Channel that September afternoon they were still confident, and justly so, that the Third Reich was winning.

The battle that day developed late in the afternoon of September 9 over the familiar landscape of southeast England. This time the Germans were unable to move across the coast without serious interruption as they had done on September 7. Two Spitfire squadrons jumped the first German formation, forcing it to drop its bombs on Canterbury rather than London. Two other British squadrons intercepted the second German force just as it crossed the coast. As the fighters tore at the German formation heading for London they were joined by a third squadron from No. 11 Group and a squadron from No. 12. The British hit the Germans hard. While the battle continued, individual German bombers began to jettison their loads over the suburbs south and southwest of London. But about ninety others pushed through to the capital. The British reckoned later that another 130 either had been forced to unload under the fighters' attacks or had bombed secondary targets. This was better. So was the ratio of losses. The Germans lost a total of twenty-eight aircraft, eighteen of which fell either in Britain or off the coast, while the British lost nineteen fighters and fourteen pilots.

Although they realized that the RAF was hard pressed, the Luftwaffe again failed to mount a second, successive heavy attack on the next day, September 10, thus repeating the pattern of September 7 and 8. But the German bombers hit hard again on the 11th.

This time about a hundred bombers fought their way through to London and bombed the dock area and the City of London. Another, small raid, possibly diversionary in intent, was made on Southampton. The scales of battle shifted. This time the Germans lost twenty-five planes, the British four more. The German command was greatly encouraged, especially because it believed the British losses to be far higher than they actually were.

During these days of maximum stress for the RAF, London and Britain, German strategic thinking was being reviewed. Hitler at the apex of the Nazi state swung from one position to another. At times he was overoptimistic, believing that the destruction of the RAF and the reduction of London were progressing at such a pace that invasion would be unnecessary. At other moments he accepted the necessity of invasion after one, big, final victory in the air. On September 11 he decided that he would not give the preliminary order for invasion before the 14th. On the 13th he announced that the moment to launch "Sea Lion" had not yet come. After this announcement he again discussed invasion with the German service commanders in chief on the 14th. This discussion led him to postpone the warning order for another three days, which meant, because of the delay between the issuance of the orders and their implementation, the postponement of the invasion until the end of the month. Such vacillation imposed a severe strain on his commanders, few of whom, as we have seen, were heart and soul in the enterprise.

The German navy, in fact, was already concerned with the increasing weight of Bomber Command's attacks upon the shipping gathered for invasion. On September 12 naval headquarters in Paris reported to Berlin:

Interruptions caused by enemy air forces, long-range artillery and light naval forces have for the first time assumed major significance. The harbors at Ostend, Dunkirk, Calais and Boulogne cannot be used as night anchorages for shipping because of the danger of English bombing and shelling. Units of the British fleet are now able to operate almost unmolested in the Channel. Owing to these difficulties, further delays are expected in the assembly of the invasion fleet.

The British naval movements that aroused the Germans' concern were the dispatch of the battleship H.M.S. *Nelson* and the battle cruiser H.M.S. *Hood* from the fleet anchorage at Scapa Flow south to Rosyth.

The receipt of the warning from the headquarters at Paris increased Hitler's doubts. He now thought that invasion should "be undertaken only as a last resort," since the necessary air supremacy "has not yet been attained." But he had not yet abandoned the idea of invasion. Hitherto Hitler's optimism, and that of many members of the High Command, had rested on the exaggerated figures of British losses retailed by the Luftwaffe. Now it was extended to include an even flimsier reason.

Talking to Halder on the 14th the Fuehrer thought that the air attacks had been "very favorable," which was correct, and that with four or five days of good weather "a decisive result will be achieved."

"We have a good chance to force England to her knees," Hitler told the Army Chief of Staff. Although decisive victory in the air might be postponed for another ten or twelve days, he thought "Britain might yet be seized by mass hysteria." It appears that at this period the propaganda spread by Dr. Goebbels about the chaos, terror and defeatism in London affected the highest levels of the party. Just then the people of London, having decided that they could expect night after night of bombing, were settling down to make the best of it.

Although he seems to have considered the idea then, Hitler decided against cancellation of the invasion. But then, as earlier, he appears extremely reluctant to launch the attack. Did he still dream that what he called "reason" would induce Churchill and his government to surrender? Did he believe the propaganda reports that mobs of hysterical Londoners were imploring the Cabinet to make peace? Whatever the cause, he agreed to postpone "Sea Lion" until September 27, the next feasible date. In the meanwhile the three fighting services began to expose the doubts they had long nursed about each other's effectiveness on the day of invasion. Field Marshal Walther von Brauchitsch, the Army Commander in Chief, informed Halder that the landing forces should be ready to invade under the protection of smoke screens if the air force was unable to smash the RAF.

Admiral Raeder, who had blown hot and cold on "Sea Lion" since early summer, had circulated, on September 14, a memorandum that provides a revealing view of professional naval opinion on the invasion at that time. The memorandum said:

(A) The present air situation does not provide conditions for carrying out the operation as the risk is still too great.

(B) If the "Sea Lion" operation fails, this will mean a great gain in prestige for the British; and the powerful effect of our attacks will be annulled.

(C) Air attacks on England, particularly on London, must continue without interruption. If the weather is favorable an intensification of the attacks is to be aimed at, without regard to "Sea Lion." The attacks must have a decisive outcome.

(D) "Sea Lion," however, must not yet be canceled, as the anxiety of the British must be kept up; if cancellation became known to the outside world, this would be a great relief to the British.

Raeder added four warnings about British strength:

(1) The preparations for a landing on the Channel coast are extensively known to the enemy, who is increasingly taking countermeasures. Symptoms are, for example, operational use of his aircraft for attacks and reconnaissances over the German operational harbors, frequent appearance of destroyers off the

south coast of England, in the Straits of Dover and on the Franco-Belgian coast, stationing of his patrol vessels off the north coast of France, Churchill's last speech, etc.

(2) The main units of the Home Fleet are being held in readiness to repel the landing, though the majority of the units are still in western bases.

(3) Already a large number of destroyers (over thirty) have been located by air reconnaissance in the southern and southeastern harbors.

(4) All available information indicates that the enemy's naval forces are solely occupied with this theater of operations.

This is a remarkable memorandum for a number of reasons. Raeder appears to have misunderstood the nature of what the Luftwaffe was trying to do. The air attacks had not succeeded to the point where invasion could be carried out. But he suggested they should be continued without interruption without regard to "Sea Lion." Had Raeder thus early come to the conclusion that, even if the RAF was driven from the skies, the presence of the British fleet still made invasion too hazardous to risk?

Certainly Raeder was aware, and Goering, von Brauchitsch and Halder were oddly ignorant, of the execution that a disciplined and confident fleet could inflict upon a mass of invasion barges. He also knew, as a member of the court, that if invasion failed there would be an immediate and bloodthirsty hunt for a scapegoat in the service. The navy lacked the towering prestige of the army. Nor did its leader enjoy, as Goering did, a close personal relationship with the Fuehrer. If things went wrong—and Raeder seems to have thought they would—he and the navy would be blamed. Goering might predict an easy passage acróss the Channel. The army might draw up ambitious plans for the occupation of England. But he, Raeder, was very doubtful.

Each of the German services by this time had completed detailed plans for its part in the invasion. But there is no evidence of co-ordinated planning such as that which preceded the great Allied landings later in the war. The German High Command, in Churchill's words, was "very far from being a co-ordinated team working together for a common purpose and with a proper understanding of each other's capabilities and limitations. Each wanted to be the brightest star in the firmament."

The army, for instance, never seems to have grasped the fact that the navy's job would not end once the first wave of invasion troops had been landed. Its generals scoffed at the admirals' fears of what the British fleet could do to the cross-Channel supply lines. The navy for its part failed to understand the reasoning behind the army's demand for a landing on the widest possible front. Neither of the older services grasped the nature of the battle the Luftwaffe was fighting while the air generals, befuddled by exaggerated statistics, tactlessly wondered why the army and navy were so slow to grasp the opportunity offered by the Luftwaffe's great victories. They had impressed Hitler. "The accomplishments of the Luftwaffe are beyond praise," he told his staff. "Four or five more days of good weather and a decisive result will be achieved." Happy in this optimism he would agree only to review the invasion question on September 17. He listened to the navy's reports of losses to the invasion fleet in the British bombing attacks but there was no indication that these affected his thinking although, as we have seen, they worried the naval authorities.

At the time it was generally agreed outside Britain that had the Germans invaded in mid-September, the defeat and subjugation of Britain would have followed rapidly and easily. Since then the evidence from both sides has given us a clearer view of what might have happened had Hitler taken the plunge.

The British intended to throw every ship, every plane and every man into the battle. The fleet was still in being. Bomber Command, although battered, remained an effective force. Fighter Command was hard pressed and weary but resourceful and determined. The army's equipment was still inferior to that of the Germans. But much new equipment had been added since Dunkirk. Of its fighting quality there could be no doubt. The country was prepared psychologically for invasion, as France had not been.

It is arguable, I believe, that the Germans might have succeeded in establishing a bridgehead under the conditions prevailing in the middle of September. They might also have been able to provide by air and sea a proportion of the necessary supplies. But continued attacks by the Royal Navy upon the lines of communication across the Channel and by the Royal Air Force upon shipping in the Continental ports, seaborne transport, and the invasion beaches would have made supply of the invading forces a hazardous and uncertain business. The techniques developed later in the war for supply by air were not known in 1940 and it is logical to assume that the use of slow German transport aircraft, like the Junkers 52, would have invited heavy losses under the guns of Fighter Command. The Germans probably would have succeeded in making a lodgment in Britain. It is highly unlikely that they would then have been able to exploit it with the rapidity and success of their European campaigns.

That period had its comic interludes, although those who remember them now recall that they did not seem particularly amusing at the time. One summer Saturday, when the watchword was "They are coming," Anthony Eden, then Secretary of State for War, snatched a day's rest at his country cottage near the Channel coast. At midday he received a telephone call from Downing Street summoning him back to London. Information from a trusted source reported that the Germans were on the way. Eden protested that a gale was blowing and that no invasion fleet could possibly put to sea in such weather. Nevertheless, he was told, he must return to London. Asking for five minutes' grace, he kept his caller on the telephone, raced out of the house and up an adjacent hill that afforded a fine view of the Channel. The gale was still blowing; if anything, the weather was worse than it had been earlier. He relayed this information to London but was told bluntly that nonetheless he must return. The information was definite. When Eden arrived in London he was met by the Prime Minister, slightly abashed. There had been a mistake in decoding. The message about invasion had been corrected with the words "for United Kingdom read Indo-China."

In the tense atmosphere of those days two stories were widely circulated. One was that the Germans had in fact attempted a landing and had been repulsed. The evidence offered was some badly burned bodies of German soldiers washed up along the south coast.

The truth, indeed, even the origin, of this tale is difficult to ascertain.

In *Their Finest Hour* Churchill wrote that the bodies were the result of either bombing or bad weather that had overtaken a German practice embarkation on the French coast: "This was the source of a widespread rumour that the Germans had attempted an invasion and had suffered very heavy losses either by drowning or by being burnt in patches of sea covered with flaming oil. We took no steps to contradict such tales, which spread freely through the occupied countries in a wildly exaggerated form and gave much encouragement to the oppressed populations."

Peter Fleming, in preparing *Operation Sea Lion*, carefully investigated the story. His conclusion was that the rumor "was wholly spontaneous, wholly baseless and wholly inexplicable." My own theory is that the bodies were not those of German soldiers but of Luftwaffe pilots who had parachuted or left a sinking bomber and that they were seen by unknown persons who spread the rumor. In the atmosphere of that time it was easy for three or four bodies to become thirty or forty.

In Germany after the war I was assured by Germans, who said they had discarded most of Dr. Goebbels's fantasies, that there had been extensive rioting against the government in London during the first weeks of the bombing.

The only incident I can recall that could be construed as a demonstration occurred one night at the Savoy Hotel. A raid had begun when a group of rather bewildered-looking people from the East End arrived at the Embankment entrance. They were led by a voluble Communist who declared they had as much right to use the Savoy's deep shelter as anyone else. This, of course, was before this man and his comrades had discovered that the Germans were "fascist hyenas." At that time they were allies of the Soviet Union fighting a war against the "Western imperialists."

In Germany, in London, in the headquarters, and on the airdromes of the Luftwaffe and Fighter Command the great battle was moving toward a climax. On September 14 the Germans again sent a force toward London. British interception was faulty and the opposition far from effective. Each force lost fourteen planes. The German High Command took heart. Perhaps the British were as badly off as the Luftwaffe claimed. The weather forecasts for the 15th were good. This was the time to put all to the test.

The British were unconscious of the approaching climax. By the middle of September the nightly bombings had priority in the public mind. The obvious weakness of the antiaircraft defense, the shortages of supplies and personnel for the shelters, and the disorganization of local governments in London aroused acrimonious dispute. In No. 10, Downing Street the Prime Minister's busy, inquisitive mind was worrying his ministers with questions arising out of the German destruction.

"How many square feet of glass have been destroyed up to date?" he asked the Home Secretary. "Can any estimate be formed? If of course our monthly production is ahead of the damage, there is no need to worry. Let me have the best estimate possible."

Life went on. People went to the movies, made love, visited friends, wrote letters. The daytime battle in the air had been going on for so long it had become almost routine. Save for the large cards saying "We are not interested in the possibilities of defeat. They do not exist," that began to appear in windows, there was no outward sign of the inner resolution. The good weather held and the parks were crowded still. People said, "What a summer it's been," and meant the weather as well as the bombing. The See p. 152 & 9. approaching Sunday, September 15, was to most Britons just another Sunday.

Chapter IX

There is a tide in the affairs of men,
Which, taken at the flood, leads on to fortune . . .

—Shakespeare

The morning was bright. In the West End the shafts of
sunlight fell on quiet, almost deserted neighborhoods. The
sirens had sounded the night before and here and there in
London men and women were mourning death and destruction. But this part of the city had been only lightly
damaged. The shop fronts, many of them even then con-
sciously old-fashioned, and the ornate buildings seemed
impervious to war and change. There were a few people
on Piccadilly, going to church, strolling in the sunshine.
The weather was like that other Sunday, a year ago, when
the war began. It was only a year but it seemed a long
time. Resignation, boredom, excitement, anxiety, remorse
had finally been replaced by a happy combination of
realism and resolution.

Few peoples have ever been treated to so much stark
realism as the British in the last days of summer, 1940.
There was an almost casual air to the three-paragraph
story on the front page of the *Sunday Times* beginning:
"Weather conditions off Dover yesterday were slightly less
favourable for any possible German invasion attempt than
for many weeks past."

There were few doubts in the public's mind that the weather would improve and the Germans would invade. An air correspondent informed his readers that "There seems little doubt that, despite that failure, invasion will be attempted—and probably very soon." The failure to which he referred was the Luftwaffe's failure to eliminate Fighter Command. The air correspondent went on to describe what was in store for the British: small groups of parachutists to "dissipate the efforts of the defence and spread alarm and confusion throughout the country." There would also, he promised, be "a big attack or a series of attacks on a frontal basis."

This prospect he described, in masterly understatement, as "unpleasant but not such as to cause undue apprehension."

The British might have been pardoned had they exhibited any of the apprehension about which the correspondent wrote so loftily. The Germans, it appeared from the newspapers, were contemplating the islanders' undoing by three separate means. The British would be invaded and beaten in the field or they would be bombed into submission or they would starve to death. The *Sunday Times* that day carried a queer little item from the Berlin correspondent of the *Basler Nachrichten* to the effect that "German official quarters" believed that Britain could be brought to her knees through the destruction of her economic life by the blockade of the U-boats, at sea, and the Luftwaffe bombing. Already, it appeared, some of the disputes within the German High Command about the feasibility of invasion had leaked to the press, perhaps intentionally.

Other statements from the German camp reported in the British press emphasized the vitality of the illusion that the British under stress might surrender. German officials in Berlin declared that London now had the choice of sharing the fate of Warsaw and/or Paris; in other words, fight on and die or surrender and survive in bondage. "London now has the chance to save itself and ward off the destiny of the German air force which will ruthlessly continue its attacks," these officials said. "The German attacks," Berlin helpfully explained, "are witness of the consciencelessness of Churchill and the British government in a war they cannot win and for which they were never morally or militarily prepared. The mass evacuation which the government has ordered constitutes simple murder. Evacution has come too late, and the people face hunger and cold in the industrialized area surrounding the capital."

Yet another agency dispatch from Berlin reported that bets being made in the Nazi capital indicated a widespread belief that the campaign against Britain would be over by the beginning of October. "Bottles of champagne" were bet, the report added, that "the campaign will end by October 15." One hopes that those who bet the battle would be over by that date were paid, even though the outcome was not as they had predicted. The propagandists of the German official news agency were busily destroying London at a rate that far outstripped the more hazardous operations of the Luftwaffe. "At a conservative estimate," it pronounced, twenty-four big docks had been burned to the ground in the week since September 7. "Despite all denials, foodstuffs are running short, the so-called voluntary evacuation of the town is growing steadily in volume and placing a big strain on the transport system which has already been greatly disorganized by the aerial attack. After eight days of attack London's armament industry has been reduced to a fraction of its former output."

Through all these and other products of inflamed imaginations and boasting nationalism spread at the time there runs a strangely plaintive note. Why don't those English give up? It's all over for them. Can't they see it? They're all alone. They can't stop us.

These sentiments were held elsewhere in the world, particularly in Eastern Europe and the Soviet Union. But in Washington the generals and admirals were beginning to grasp the idea that morale, civilian as well as military, counts for something in total war. The War Department was rather belatedly recognizing that the Luftwaffe's invincibility was a myth, although final opinions were reserved until the invasion began. At the State Department the feeling developed that Ambassador Kennedy's predictions of inevitable defeat for Britain might be a bit too gloomy. The *New York Times* and other important eastern newspapers with an interest in international affairs were beginning to understand that the resistance of the British people had changed the character of the war. A *Times* editorial commented:

How long, one wonders, can the civilians of London stand it? It seems incredible that human flesh and blood and human sanity can endure these things, yet London civilians have endured them with a courage that compels the admiration of everyone in the world who still values freedom.

As the terrible climax draws near the British are neither crippled nor cowed. They should be doubly able to withstand it, because they know, to the last man, woman and child, what freedom means.

Meanwhile many Londoners, interested, and casually grateful for this transatlantic praise, were strolling in twos and threes toward Buckingham Palace where a time bomb, dropped on Friday, had exploded on Saturday. They thought American moral support encouraging but rather like praise for a child who has been brave on a trip to the dentist. They knew a climax was coming in which praise or blame from abroad would have no effect. Almost everyone knew someone who had seen the bodies of German soldiers on a beach or had heard about an abortive parachute drop in the Midlands or South Wales. It was impossible now to get away from the war; every news item on the front page of the *Sunday Times* had referred to some aspect of it. Reading the reports they might appear to need the nerve tonic, glowingly praised in an advertisement, as a means of building "energy reserves." As incurable zoophiles, however, they applauded the establishment of a large voluntary service to treat any of the country's million-odd pets and livestock hurt during the raids. Sports lovers were having a thin time. Soccer matches had been interrupted on Saturday by air raids and the indefatigable D. R. Gent in the *Sunday Times* was doing his best to arrange informal rugby matches. In the same newspaper the racing correspondent, "Fairway," hoped that the Luftwaffe would "not cause a complete cessation of racing for the remainder of the war, for this would deal the bloodstock industry a blow from which it might never recover. . . . No good purpose can be served in allowing this industry to decay if it can be found possible to preserve it." The advertisement columns offered a wide choice for those already seeking a "safe hotel" away from the bombing. "A Haven of Rest," "Safe and Sunny," "Peaceful Nights," said the headlines advertising hideaways in Devon and Cornwall. Those who stayed in London were assured they could "dine and dance in safety" in the new underground restaurant at Grosvenor House, while other hotels had added "Air Raid Shelter" to the familiar "All Modern Conveniences." Another advertisement, more to the point of those parlous times, asked, on behalf of government, those living in the country near military camps to offer the soldiers or airmen hospitality, to save old books and magazines, and to allow them the use of the bathtub if necessary. This, it was pointed out, was a "small return for all they are doing." That Sunday neither the advertisement for "excellent woollen dresses" at four guineas nor the appearance of Edward G. Robinson in *The Silver Bullet* was likely to divert the Londoners from the point. This was, an editorialist pointed out, that for Britain "after months of waiting the ordeal is upon her now. Beyond it lies victory, if she holds fast."

The early morning had been misty and cool at most of the fighter airfields. A pilot, out early, marked the first turning of the leaf in a copse off the airfield and saw beyond the placid rich fields. England, he concluded, with all her faults "was definitely worth fighting for." But there was little time for such introspection. By now the days were melting into one another. There were no Sundays or Saturdays. Sometimes forty-eight hours' leave. "God, you look forward to it for a week, you think of a booze-up or a popsie and when it comes you're so damned tired all you want to do is sleep." They were fighting one of the great battles of history. But for them it was made up of small, highly personal things. September 7 was not the day "the Jerries went for London" so much as the day "Tommy bought it over Southend." The fighter pilots were counting the cost now. The cost in dead friends. The cost in Tim or Nigel lying in hospital with new eyelids and new lips grafted on to burned faces. The mental agony of gazing at a blank sheet of paper and mustering courage to write letters to parents or girl friends. It was then one realized how young they were. An anguished voice asking: "How in Christ's name do you tell them? He was burning all the way down. Oh, muck the Germans and muck the bloody war." Now, as the sun brushed the mists from the fields of England and lit the sleepy villages, they swallowed scalding tea and moved to their machines. It had been going on since June. Once again they were ready.

There was a stir across the Channel too. The Reichsmarschall had ordered a full-scale attack on London. The air crews digested their breakfasts thinking, as all men do at such times, of what a near thing it had been with that Spitfire over the coast the last time or writing letters home. They were not much different from those other young men in England. But they had begun this long battle full of confidence in a swift and certain victory; inspired by their own successes, willing to believe those boastful voices from Berlin. "They were different in September," a German captain of infantry recalled. "Quieter, more serious. Oh, they could laugh, yes, and they made jokes. But the battle was not a joke. They told us 'you in the army have it easy. This is the Luftwaffe's war.'" Some, outwardly confident, nursed doubts about equipment.

Adolf Galland complained that the new tactics forced his fighters to fly "straight-and-level" with the slower, less maneuverable bombers, thus abandoning to the RAF the "advantages of surprise, initiative, height, speed and, above all, the fighting spirit and aggressive attitude which marks all successful fighter squadrons." In his book *The First and the Last* Galland recalls that when he protested against these tactics Goering asked, "Well, major, what kind of fighters would you like?"

"Reichsmarschall, give me a squadron of Spitfires" was the answer.

Galland and other German fliers noted, too, that the British always seemed better informed about the weather, that radar gave them "superbinoculars" that could see across the Channel. Even by September 15 the bomber crews were complaining that the intensification of antiaircraft fire over London made accurate bombing very difficult. But they complained to themselves. For in Berlin Dr. Goebbels was making mincemeat out of London night after night.

All that summer the Luftwaffe had been correct. They had tried to make friends with the French and the Belgians and the Dutch. They had played with the children. Big farm boys from Bavaria and Lower Saxony had helped the farmers in the fields. Pilots from the cities of the Ruhr and Berlin had borrowed horses and ridden along the white, dusty roads. They had told the people in the villages and the farmhouses that the war would soon be over and they would soon go home.

They did not go home. There, too, old friends died. There, too, the pressure was endless. Older officers, who remembered the Kaiser's war and the first giddy weeks of success, wondered whether, despite all that was said in Berlin, this, too, might not develop into a long, exhausting war. They were bombing London, all right. At night the bomber crews could see the fires of London still when they crossed the coast on the return journey. But the English were stubborn. The old men remembered 1918.

Now they were poised for another great attack. The Heinkel 111's, the Dornier 17's, the Junkers 88's rose from their fields at Montdidier and Clairmont, from Saint-Léger and Cambrai, from Eindhoven, Brussels, Lille and Beauvais. As they gained height, heavy-bellied with bombs, the Messerschmitt 109's and 110's came to join them from Saint-Omer, Laon, Wissant, from Amiens,

Guyancourt, Crécy-en-Ponthieu, Ligescourt and Alençon.
As the squadrons headed for the coast the peasants, trudg-
ing in their best black to Mass, paused to watch. Far away
in England the radar sets began to register their approach.
They were headed for London but before they reached
the capital they must cross the same old battlefield, the
area about eighty miles long, thirty-eight broad and from
five to six miles high over southeast England where most
of the fighting had taken place since the battle began.

On the British airdromes the pilots observed that the
weather had "duffed up," that is, thick, low cloud was developing and there was a certain amount of ground haze.
The early morning had been relatively quiet. Now, as the
German formations crossed the Channel, Fighter Command rose again to meet them. Some who watched them
thought of the words from Henry V: "Once more unto the
breach, dear friends, once more . . ." The battle that was
to try Fighter Command to the limits of its resources had
reached its climax. The history of the world would depend
on those Spitfires and Hurricanes climbing overhead.

The Germans planned a series of raids on London by
bombers of Luftflotte II and subsidiary attacks on Portland and the Supermarine Works, where Spitfires were
made, outside Southampton. Goering hoped to provide
five fighters for every bomber. In the event, the Germans
flew around 700 fighter sorties that day. Kesselring, at
Goering's orders, had made special efforts to ensure
methodical assembly of bombers and their fighter escorts.
The consequent slowness with which the raids developed

helped to give the British ample warning of the approach of the raid. The British fighter squadrons that had been at "superreadiness," that is, with pilots waiting in the cockpits, took off when radar began to report formations of "sixty plus" and "seventy plus" over the European coast.

That morning I was at No. 11 Group headquarters at Uxbridge. As the reports of the German concentrations began to come in, Park listened with complete equanimity. "There'll be someone along to meet them," he remarked. The headquarters had a businesslike air but there was also an almost tangible feeling of excitement and perhaps strain. So many things could go wrong. There were so many errors that could be made. Battles are a compound of errors, someone said. That day the errors were on the German side. The British were quick to take advantage of them. But in the morning all was in the balance.

Around the huge map table young men and women of the RAF and WAAF stood gazing at the map, fingering disks representing squadrons. Facing them was an enormous blackboard divided into six columns. Each column stood for a sector station of the group and was subdivided into sections for each squadron controlled by the station. Electric bulbs indicated which squadrons were at readiness, standing by or available; in other words, whether they were ready to take off in two, five or twenty minutes. Officers, most of whom had been in the battle since the beginning, weighed the information passed to them from the radar stations and from the Observer Corps, whose members, equipped with field glasses and telephones, provided information on the German formations once they had crossed the English coast.

The first German error was the time taken to assemble the bomber and fighter forces. This was compounded by the decision to divide the main attack into two phases. The interval between the attacks gave the British squadrons, which had to refuel after just over an hour in the air, time to land, refuel and rearm, and take off again. Nor on that day did the Germans make the feints which in the past had forced Park to send squadrons away from the main battle area. Perhaps they were too confident. At any rate, by eleven o'clock it was clear that the Luftwaffe was mounting a major attack. Fighter Command by then had seventeen squadrons in the air, eleven from No. 11 Group, five from No. 12 Group, and one from No. 10 Group. These were the wheelhorses of Fighter Command, the squadrons Dowding had striven to maintain in the front line, the bone and sinew of the defense: among them the Hurricanes of 17 and 73 Squadrons, the County of Gloucester Squadron, 501; the Poles of 303 Squadron, the Spitfires of 603. They flew from the airfields for which they had fought in August and early September: Biggin Hill and North Weald and Hornchurch. From Duxford in the north came the five squadrons from No. 12 Group, 611 from West Lancashire; 242 Squadron led by the legless, indomitable Douglas Bader to whom Air Vice-Marshal Leigh-Mallory had given general supervision of the five squadrons. Leigh-Mallory was a firm believer in large concentrations of fighters and in head-on, diving tactics to break up enemy formations. Now he sent nearly sixty aircraft south into the battle just beginning over the coast.

Park was not so devoted to what later became known as the "big wing" tactics as was Leigh-Mallory. But ten of the eleven squadrons put up by No. 11 Group were deployed in pairs. Aware of the German approach and in good if not overwhelming strength, Fighter Command had obvious advantages over the invaders. Soon after the first German formations had crossed the coast they were hit by a whirlwind of British fighters. Two Spitfire squadrons jumped the Luftwaffe force over Canterbury. Three more squadrons entered the battle. From that first wild encounter a Spitfire pilot recalled:

"The Jerry flattened out and I pulled up on him and gave him a real burst. He just dropped through the cloud and I had to pull out and look for more. I stooged around in the cloud at reasonable speed and then saw the wreckage of the Jerry, an Me 109, burning at a hell of a clip as it fell. I climbed up through the cloud and just missed colliding with a Ju 88 which was on fire and being worried by Hurricanes. Then suddenly the sky ahead was absolutely clear. Not an aircraft in sight. Then I saw below another Jerry formation. I dived hard on one Ju 88 and gave him a three-second burst. Didn't think it would do the trick. I closed again when suddenly he turned over and I could see he was burning badly. They were calling me on R/T and I turned toward the rest of the squadron. Another Hun formation was coming in and we climbed to get altitude. Above the bombers I saw Me 109's and Me 110's. It was damned hot and my arms were tired."

Park was not satisfied with his original reception committee. He committed six more squadrons, which had been in reserve until that point, to the battle. The crowds who were watching the battle from the ground all over southeast England saw that for once there seemed to be enough British fighters to do the job. At No. 11 Group headquarters they were not so sure.

Two of these six squadrons sailed into the leading German formation as it neared the Medway. The Germans pushed on, taking their losses but flying steadily and reforming whenever a bomber fell out. They had no rest. Just before the formation reached London it was attacked again, this time by four Hurricane squadrons. While the German fighters and bombers were engaging this force, they were suddenly struck by the five squadrons from No. 12 Group. The three Hurricane squadrons of this group took on the German bombers while the two Spitfire formations attacked the escorting fighters.

The British had been climbing on the way down, moving above the cloud to 20,000 feet plus. The black blossoms of antiaircraft fire directed the fighters toward the Germans. Again the Germans had erred. Contrary to Goering's instructions, their fighters were so high above the bombers that they left the latter virtually unprotected. The Hurricanes' onslaught broke up the German formations. The Dorniers and Ju 88's headed for cloud cover with the British in pursuit. Plumes of black smoke from burning bombers marked the sky. Under this pressure, heavier and more sustained than any they had ever encountered, the German bombers jettisoned their loads. Bombs fell in eastern and southeastern London and in the suburbs. Two bridges were hit, more apparently by luck than by accurate bombing. Another bomb, which did not explode, fell in the grounds of Buckingham Palace. The German formation, badly mauled, swung homeward only to encounter four fresh Hurricane squadrons over Kent and Sussex. Then suddenly it was quiet.

The fighter squadrons returned to their bases. Time for something to eat, a cup of tea, fuel and ammunition. They were too warwise in Fighter Command to be jubilant. But as the intelligence officers gathered their reports from the returning fliers they realized that the battle had gone their way. The German errors were not so easy to perceive then. What the British did see was that with enough fighters concentrated and with attacks delivered by two or more squadrons at once, no important German formation would be able to get through to London without serious losses. Yet it was still early afternoon. The day was not done.

The second German attack developed in midafternoon. Again the target was London and for the second time the Luftwaffe began the attack without trying to feint the defenders out of position. This time Park's headquarters did not get quite as much warning from radar as it had in the morning. Still there was enough time to get twelve squadrons, in six pairs, into position while the first wave of the German force was over the Channel. Before the

German formations had crossed the coast, another seven and one-half squadrons were thrown in by No. 11 Group. To this force No. 12 Group added its five squadrons, still flying as a single formation, and No. 10 Group sent a single squadron from the west. Twenty-five and one-half squadrons; a big force. The old firm was in business again.

The Germans divided their attacking force that afternoon into three formations. The first of these encountered trouble almost immediately in the shape of two Spitfire squadrons from Hornchurch. The Spitfires were soon joined by a flight of Hurricanes. The second formation ran into Hurricanes from Tangmere. In this engagement the British fighters attacked so fiercely that for the first time that day a part of the German formation turned back toward the sea and safety, dropping bombs as it retired. The remainder of the force plowed on toward London across a sky dotted with antiaircraft bursts and marked by the vapor trails of British squadrons hurrying to the battle.

The Germans who flew steadily on toward London collided over the capital with fresh Hurricane squadrons from Northolt. Once again some of the bombers turned back. But those that remained fought a full-scale battle that raged from the heart of London westward. Just before three o'clock ten squadrons from No. 11 Group and the five-squadron wing from No. 12 were all in action. This was the peak of the battle.

In the curiously impersonal warfare of the air nothing occurred in the battle itself to mark its peak. For pilots there was the familiar sensation of flying in and out of chaos filled with bombers and fighters wheeling, climbing, turning. Flashes of orange flame. Clouds of smoke drifting across windscreens. A Hurricane engages an Me 110, another German jumps the Hurricane. A Spitfire pilot closing a Ju 88 sees a stream of tracer going over one wing. He pulls out, climbs, makes his pass at an Me 109. Smoke pours from the German fighter's engine. Slowly, almost deliberately, it turns over and begins to fall. More tracer and three Me 109's diving. The Spitfire heads for the clouds. The pilot comes out, looks down, and sees the sea far below. Far to the east a lone Ju 88 heads for France and safety. Faintly through the R/T comes the call "All aircraft return to base and land." No sign that this had been a decisive moment of a decisive battle.

So hotly had the Germans been engaged that the damage to London from their bombs was negligible. Once again there had been some lucky hits scattered over a wide area. But no single section of the capital had suffered as badly as had the Thames-side communities on September 7. Even to the southwest, where their initial luck had been better, the Germans had failed to score a significant success.

The raid on Portland was carried out by German bombers alone, tactics that on the results of the day's fighting thus far seem foolhardy. Yet so incalculable is war that the attack might have come off. True, the radar chain picked up the attacking force as it crossed the Channel. But, as so often happened in those days, the radar operators underestimated the strength of the formations. The raiders came in from an unexpected direction and took the defenses almost entirely by surprise. One antiaircraft gun emplacement and one squadron of fighters were all that the defenders could bring to bear on the attack and the fighters did not make contact until after the Germans had bombed. But the bombing was inaccurate; little damage was done to the naval dockyard at Portland.

If the great crisis of the battle passed without recognition among those fighting it in the air, it was clearly visible at No. 11 Group headquarters. Park had a distinguished visitor that day, for the Prime Minister had driven over from Chequers to watch the course of the battle. At the height of the battle Churchill noted that, despite the Air Vice-Marshal's apparent calmness, all the fighter squadrons available were in the air, not a single squadron was left in reserve. At this point in the battle Park called Dowding at Stanmore, Fighter Command headquarters, and asked for three more squadrons from No. 12 Group to be placed at his disposal to meet any new attack that might develop while the squadrons already in action were refueling and rearming. Churchill noticed a growing air of strain:

"Hitherto I have watched in silence. I now asked 'What other reserves have we?' 'There are none,' said Air Vice-Marshal Park. In an account which he wrote about it afterwards he said that at this I 'looked grave.' Well I might."

So Churchill, from his own account in *Their Finest Hour*, knew that the crisis was at hand. I have often wondered since if, in that hour, he thought back to May 16 when he had stood with another commander, General Gamelin, Commander in Chief of the Allied forces, asked a similar question, and received a similar answer. Churchill then asked "Ou est la masse de manœuvre?" and received in reply the single word "Aucune." This time, too, there were no reserves available. But this time the defense stood firm. As the Prime Minister and the Air Marshal talked the Germans, badly battered, began to withdraw from London. The disks on the huge map in the operations room moved eastward.

That was the last major action of the day. Just about six o'clock a small force of bombers and fighters managed to slip past the five squadrons guarding the Hampshire coast and bomb the area around Southampton. The Germans drew off worried by the fighters and the day was over. Here and there on the hills and fields of southern England the wreckage of aircraft, most of them Germans, burned and smoldered through the twilight and into the night. The people who had watched all day for glimpses of the fighting, who had seen fighters and bombers plummeting to earth, who had heard the shrill staccato of machine guns and the pop-pop-pop of cannon in the air above them went home. The nights were drawing in and there was time for tea before "the news" on the BBC. In the pubs men concluded that "Jerry had been given a good knock."

This indeed was true. Fighter Command shot down fifty-six invading aircraft and the gunners of the antiaircraft got four more. The loss to the British was twenty-six aircraft. On analysis the figures represent not only a serious reverse to the Germans in numbers of aircraft shot down but a serious blow to their tactical scheme. Goering had committed 123 bombers to the battle and assigned close to 700 fighters as escort. But thirty-four bombers, or nearly a third of those engaged, had been shot down despite an escort ratio of approximately five to one. Clearly the close escort tactics could not protect the bombers. And if Goering reversed his tactics and allowed the fighters more latitude in their dispositions, the Hurricanes undoubtedly would find the bombers easier game and the losses would mount. The Germans were perplexed. In the minds of the Luftwaffe commanders, as in the air above southern England, the tide had turned.

But the day battle now was only a part, albeit the decisive part, of the much larger battle that continued on through the night. While the fighter pilots lounged in quiet groups discussing the day's events, those of Bomber Command were being briefed for the night's operations. Their targets were the familiar ports across the Channel with their swarms of transports and barges. Carrying the maximum bomb load, for the distance was short, the Whitleys, Hampdens, Blenheims, Battles and Wellingtons swept across the Channel. We know these attacks already were worrying the German naval high command. Its concern was soundly based for, in the two weeks of attacks that began on the night of September 15, Bomber Command destroyed or crippled 12 per cent of the German invasion fleet. To anyone familiar with the immense intricacy of mounting an invasion, it is obvious that the damage to the ships was only the start. Every successful attack by the RAF meant the revision of loading schedules, changes in the operational plan for crossing the Channel, and finally and most unwelcome to the army, alterations in the order of battle for invasion.

Night after night the "invasion coast" was lit by fires. Pilots saw wooden jetties, intended for nothing larger than fishing boats, disintegrate under their bombs. The supplies so carefully gathered and carried such long distances from Germany for the invasion disappeared in fires easily visible from the English coast. The troops assembled for the great enterprise were hurried to the coast in the daytime to help clear the rubble. For the German defenders radar did not exist. So each night there was the shocking surprise of a British bomber formation sweeping in over the sea, the first sticks of bombs and fires started before the German antiaircraft fire could become effective. The Royal Navy ventured south to shell four of the Channel ports. Eight barges were destroyed at Ostend. The waterfront at Boulogne burned for fifteen hours. An ammunition train was blown up behind Calais. The small ports were disorganized just as parts of London had been. But because they were small, the attacks had a total effect much greater than the widely scattered raids on the huge British capital.

For London was still under attack. On the night of September 15 there were 181 German bombers over the city. They dropped 224 tons of high explosive and 279 canisters of incendiary bombs. These fell on a city and a people immensely buoyed by the news of the fighting that day. The Air Ministry had announced that 185 Germans had been brought down; the greatest "day" in the whole battle. The discrepancy between this figure and the real German loss of sixty—fifty-six to fighters, four to antiaircraft guns— is inexplicable. Inevitably during major engagements, like those of September 15, fighting became confused and spread over a wide area. Pilots innocently claimed the same aircraft shot down. Often, too, German planes thought to be destroyed made it back to France. The Air Ministry, of course, was under heavy pressure to reveal the claims of German planes destroyed or damaged as soon as possible. Had there been more time for checking, a more accurate figure might have been announced. Certainly that winter officers of the RAF said privately that perhaps the German losses on the big days of the Battle of Britain perhaps were lower than had been claimed at the time. Again, we must set against the exaggeration the lift these figures gave to the morale of a population fighting for its life alone against what had appeared to be the overwhelming power of the Third Reich. The conviction then, and earlier in the battle, that the RAF was not only winning but winning decisively was a remarkable tonic to people starved of success. It is worth noting in this connection that experienced military observers at the time saw nothing extraordinary in the British claims. Brigadier General Strong, head of the United States Military Mission to Britain, returning to New York on September 19, reported that the British claims of German aircraft losses were "on the conservative side." This from an officer of a service that three months earlier had been convinced of the Luftwaffe's invincibility.

In retrospect these exaggerations appear to have harmed the Germans more than they did the British. The figures of German losses reported to the Air Ministry by Fighter Command were sometimes two or two and a half times as great as the actual German losses. But this did not breed overconfidence. The British knew that Fighter Command was still outnumbered by the Luftwaffe. All the intelligence reports indicated that aircraft production in Germany was well ahead of that in the United Kingdom. The British could barely afford their losses. The Germans at the crux of the battle in the first two weeks of September still could.

The Germans, however, were twice deluded. They exaggerated the British losses. But they did worse. In their interservice reports they falsified their own losses and exaggerated the damage done to British cities and ports and to RAF installations. At the time it was thought in Britain that the patently false claims broadcast by Berlin were for German and European consumption and were intended as a morale builder, although why German morale should need nourishing no one quite knew. The real figures of German losses and an estimate of British losses closer to the truth, the British believed, were known to the Oberkommando Wehrmacht and the chiefs of the fighting services. The Luftwaffe High Command may have known the true picture. But it is highly doubtful if the army or the navy was given the facts. Such duplicity is common to totalitarian nations in times of stress. During the battles of 1941 the Russian propagandists told lies faster than a horse could trot.

The last German night raiders flew eastward in the early morning of September 16. As the dawn broke the columns of smoke arose over London and over the battered invasion ports. In the capital the sirens were silent and the streets echoed to the usual early-morning sounds. Men came downstairs in their pajamas to seize the newspapers and read the tremendous news: "185 SHOT DOWN AND MORE TO COME," said one headline. Across the Channel the German army turned out in the misty early morning for more invasion exercises. In the hangars and repair shops of the RAF and the Luftwaffe weary mechanics slipped outside for a smoke in early light. Another day. The war was still there. But from September 15 onward it would never be the same again.

Chapter X

The Londoners were very brave, and they went on being brave for a long time.

—PETER FLEMING

The Germans are a brave and stubborn people. In 1918 and 1945 they displayed a sullen valor in defeat. Their weakness in war is a tendency to exaggerate their own successes. For many reasons, some of them explicable, some of them lost in the complexities of Hitler's mind, this was their most dangerous failing during the Battle of Britain. Now, in the second half of September, reality, harsh and cold, overtook the High Command. The outcome of the fighting on Sunday, September 15, awoke the sleepwalkers in Berlin. They had to face three facts. The first and most immediately apparent was that a major attack on London had cost a total of sixty aircraft, the majority bombers. The second was that Fighter Command, far from being on the edge of defeat, had reacted to the German challenge by massing an unprecedented number of Spitfires and Hurricanes which had attacked the German squadrons with their customary headlong ferocity. Finally the bombers that had been able to get through to London had been so harried by the defenders that the attack, when it was delivered, was haphazard. It might have helped to weaken the will to resist of the people of the capital and we know there were some Germans who saw this as one of the objectives of the bombing. But considered as the type of strategic bombing that prepared for invasion the operation was a failure.

On the basis of a single day's fighting the results of September 15 might not have appeared so conclusive from the German side. But Kesselring and Sperrle, the Luftflotte commanders most concerned, were forced to regard that day's fighting as forming part of a generally depressing pattern. Since the attacks on London in strength had begun on September 7 the Luftwaffe had lost more than two hundred aircraft—these included nine destroyed on Continental airfields by British "intruder" bombing—and over half the planes lost were bombers. This was a serious cumulative loss to an air force that had been extensively engaged almost uninterruptedly since May.

The defeat of September 15 had another effect, less evident at the time but perhaps more far-reaching in its influence upon the war. The confidence of the Luftwaffe, which had been slightly shaken by its inability to drive the British from the air in the earlier stages of the battle, now ebbed. Even before that memorable day German fighter pilots had grumbled that the tactics of close fighter escort reduced their ability to cope with the British fighters. In the encounters of the 15th the fighter pilots often found that to maintain close escort it was necessary to fly eccentric courses that took them away from their charges. Since British fighters during the battle had been able to jump German bomber formations while the fighters were outside the battle area, relations between the bomber crews and their supposed protectors were far from happy. The German fighter pilots had a justifiably high opinion of their own skill and of their aircraft, especially the Me 109. But, although this opinion was supported by the High Command, the bomber remained more important to the leaders than the fighters. This was understandable. The Germans were on the offensive and only the bomber could administer the punishment to Britain that could knock out the RAF's bomber and fighter bases or batter the British into submission.

These reflections on the course of the fighting in September were added to and complicated by a number of other factors in the minds of the German strategists. It was now apparent that the Luftwaffe could not get to London, quite apart from bombing it effectively, by daylight without paying an exorbitant price. Consequently, to press the last phase of the German daytime air offensive would mean the gradual destruction of the Luftwaffe, particularly its bombers. The bombers were precious to Goering, Sperrle and Kesselring, who saw them as the Luftwaffe's means of dealing effective, even decisive blows during the remainder of the war. But they were also precious to the ground generals like von Brauchitsch and Halder, who considered the bomber a type of very long-range artillery and consequently an indispensable part of the German army's equipment. They were not particularly happy about air operations that might waste these important machines and their trained crews without, as far as they could see, dealing a knockout blow to the RAF.

Another factor in German service thinking at that moment was the profound differences that existed about the feasibility of Operation "Sea Lion." The fears of the Navy High Command have been cited. But in mid-September the army, possibly shaken by the failure of the Luftwaffe to secure that often-promised air supremacy, began to have second thoughts about the invasion. Daily contact with the sea by divisional, corps and army commanders along the European coast had been instructive. They began to recognize what an intractible, unpredictable element it was. At the same time they had the dubious pleasure of listening, night after night, to prolonged British bombing attacks each of which destroyed embarkation facilities, supplies and transports. Disillusionment and doubt, not perhaps quite so strong as that prevailing in the navy, began to trouble the hitherto unworried army.

It is impossible to escape the impression that to Hitler and his court the doubts expressed by professional soldiers of the highest qualifications were almost welcome. The defeat of September 15 caught the Fuehrer at a moment when he was wavering. As we have seen, on September 11 he decided to withhold the preliminary order to start "Sea Lion" before the 14th. On the 13th he declared that the moment to begin the operation had not come. On the 14th he discussed the situation again with his senior commanders and decided to postpone issuing the warning orders for another three days. This meant that the invasion could not begin until September 27. After that it would have to wait until October 8 for favorable tides. This would bring the operation into the autumn months when the Channel is notoriously rough, an important factor when soldiers unaccustomed to sea voyages have to cross water, land in the face of determined opposition, and fight.

What were the chief influences upon Hitler's mind? Certainly the failure of the Luftwaffe to achieve air supremacy was an important one, although here, as in much else, it is well to remember that the Fuehrer, like the army and navy commanders, made his estimates on the basis of highly exaggerated Luftwaffe claims. The British victory of September 15 could reasonably have been dismissed by them as a last desperate effort by an already defeated air force. The second influence which seems to have gripped Hitler's mind was his belief in a cheap victory. At one time he had believed that a single German bombing attack on London would drive the people in panic from the capital and block the roads. The German propagandists with ears well attuned to what their leader liked to hear fed this belief with their tall tales of chaos and evacuation. The order of September 14 that put "Sea Lion" back to the end of the month spoke, for instance, of continuing the Luftwaffe attacks against important military and civilian objectives "as long as there are worthwhile targets," a clear indication that Hitler believed his own publicity. These words "imply a belief," according to Peter Fleming's study of the period, "that everything worth destroying in

[211]

London was already within measurable distance of being destroyed."

Since no one knows what actually went on in Hitler's mind and since he was an adept at duplicity, it would be incautious to accept as fact the assumption that he abandoned invasion because he believed that the war could be won by other means. This assumption, however, is supported by yet another factor in German calculations. During June, July and August the British lost 631,939 tons and the Allies 291,184 tons of merchant shipping to German U-boats and surface raiders. September was even more fruitful for the German navy. It sunk a total of 403,211 tons or more than half the total of the preceding three months. The U-boats' September successes—131,202 tons in the first two weeks—were already being reported to the Fuehrer when he was deciding on the future of Operation "Sea Lion." They cannot help but have had a powerful effect upon his mind. Postwar analyses of World War I had revealed that the German submarine offensive of 1916–17 had almost defeated the Royal Navy. If that prize had been so nearly within the grasp of a German force armed with the comparatively puny U-boats of the First War, how much more promising was the present situation when the U-boats were larger and faster, were able to remain at sea much longer, and enjoyed the use of a string of bases along the western coast of Europe from Bordeaux in the south to the North Cape in the north. Churchill regarded the Battle of the Atlantic, the longest battle of the war, as a prime source of British concern.

Hitler may have seen the sea offensive in September 1940 as one part of a combined offensive, the nightly bombing of London being the other, that would force Britain to sue for peace.

This is conjecture. The fact is that the war diary at German naval headquarters on September 17 records: "The enemy air force is still by no means defeated; on the contrary, it shows increasing activity. The weather situation as a whole does not permit us to expect a period of calm" —in the Channel. "The Fuehrer therefore decides to postpone 'Sea Lion' indefinitely." There must have been sighs of relief in many operational headquarters of the army and the navy. There certainly would have been even more heartfelt sighs in Britain had the decision been known.

The invasion was postponed after it had been clearly demonstrated that, although the Luftwaffe might occasionally mount successful bombing attacks against individual targets, it could not drive the British from the skies. Fighter Command and Bomber Command were still in being as experienced services fighting with growing confidence. Air supremacy, which the Luftwaffe considered necessary to successful invasion, remained remote if not entirely unattainable. The Germans had lost the daylight battle of the air. Consequently, they could not launch an invasion without running risks that no commander or political leader, not even the chief of a totalitarian state, would dare to take. Hitler, admittedly, ran great risks in launching the invasion of the Soviet Union. But at the time these were not apparent in Berlin. In 1940, however, the penalties were apparent: bombing of the invading forces by an unshaken RAF, fighter squadrons to frustrate the Luftwaffe's very long-range artillery, a navy rested and refurbished since Dunkirk, an army fighting with its traditional tenacity on its own fatherland, a civilian population roused and led by a man of determined genius. All these counted now. None of them would have counted had Fighter Command been beaten.

September 15, or the nearest Sunday, is celebrated in Britain as Battle of Britain day, a day of thanksgiving for deliverance. There is good reason for this observance. For the RAF on that day, in 1940, delivered the country from the gravest peril it had known since Napoleon massed the Grande Armée at Boulogne.

Hitler's decision, of course, was hidden from the British. Sensibly the Germans were at some pains to disguise the facts. The majority of the ground forces and equipment selected for invasion remained where they were. British reconnaissance planes, however, reported the gradual dispersal of the barges and transports gathered in the five principal coastal ports. The number of vessels declined from 1,004 on September 18 to 448 in the last week of October. From the German naval records it is clear that this dispersal was not exclusively the consequence of Hitler's decision to postpone the invasion but of a natural desire to prevent further losses. By that time 214 barges and twenty-one transports had been sunk or severely damaged by the British bombers. But the British could not be certain that this dispersal meant the abandonment of invasion. The dispersal might be a rational movement to cut German losses. Their thinking, in fact, was what Hitler wished it to be. He had postponed the invasion. But he wanted to maintain the threat of invasion. Was this part of his persistent illusion that the British would crack under threats and pressure?

The landing fleet was dispersed but both it and the troops it was to carry were kept in a state of readiness until October 12, when the invasion operation was postponed, not indefinitely but until the spring of 1941 by the following order:

Supreme Command   Fuehrer's Headquarters
Top Secret   12/10/1940

1) The Fuehrer has decided that from now until the spring, preparations for "Sea Lion" shall be continued solely for the purpose of maintaining political and military pressure on England.

Should the invasion be reconsidered in the spring or early summer of 1941, orders for a renewal of operational readiness will be issued later. In the meantime military conditions for a later invasion are to be improved.

(Signed) KEITEL

It is interesting to note that the day after Hitler postponed invasion indefinitely, September 18, the Fuehrer's headquarters issued the famous Directive No. 21 for Operation "Barbarossa," which began: "The German Armed Forces must be prepared even before the end of the war against England to overthrow Soviet Russia in a rapid campaign . . ." Like Directive No. 16 dealing with the invasion of Britain, this too was a dream. As Charles de

Gaulle, then an obscure staff officer, had written six years before, the German people are inclined to "vast ambitions."

One of the most curious aspects of Hitler's equivocation about the invasion of Britain is the manner in which some great blow against his chief enemies kept recurring in his thoughts later. Planning for the attack on Russia had already begun when, later in 1940, he startled his advisers by talking in his rambling way about an invasion of Ireland. In January of 1941 General Kurt Student, the ablest of the German commanders of airborne troops, was summoned to Berlin to discuss the invasion of Ireland by air. Did Hitler see this operation as the first phase of the invasion of Britain itself or as a further step toward the strangulation of Britain by cutting her seaborne life lines and bombing her ports? The invasion and occupation of Ireland would not have been a difficult operation in the initial stages. Once established there, the Germans would have been in a favorable position to attack the shipping that flowed into Britain's west coast ports around the northern and southern coasts of Ireland. But as was customary with Hitler, and indeed with some of his ablest military commanders, he discounted the difficulties of maintaining a force overseas. German naval headquarters spent some anxious moments that winter preparing papers to show just how difficult this would be in the face of the Royal Navy. The beguiling prospect of a cheap victory over Britain through a combination of U-boats and bombers remained with Hitler long after the invasion had been postponed.

The air attack on Britain therefore was maintained by day and night although daytime attacks were less numerous, partly because of the beating the Luftwaffe had taken between September 7 and September 15 and partly because of increasingly bad weather. The bravery and persistence of the Germans in the war in the air never shone brighter than in those days of late September when pilots and aircrews, professionally aware of the strength and determination of Fighter Command, returned to the attack on London although in greatly reduced strength. The raids were smaller in terms of the total number of aircraft used. And to protect the bombers the proportion of bombers to fighters was again reduced. London by October was being attacked by small formations of fighter-bombers escorted by fighters. The Ju 88, which was unpopular with aircrews, was employed almost invariably when bombers were needed.

The British were perplexed by these tactics. Fighters and fighter-bombers flew faster than bombers and fighter escort, so No. 11 Group got less warning from radar than it had earlier in the year. And radar, of course, could not distinguish between types of aircraft, so that the controllers on the ground had difficulty in selecting the German force that carried bombs and would thus do the maximum damage if it got through. Indeed with German fighters coming in at great heights—the Me 109 had a better performance above 25,000 feet than the early Spitfires and Hurricanes—radar had great difficulty in picking up the raiders at all. If the British were perplexed, they were also experienced. Fighters, usually Spitfires, were ordered to patrol at great height to spot incoming German formations and report their approach to No. 11 Group headquarters. This was a start. But it was not until Park ordered patrols by two squadrons whenever the weather favored high flying by the Germans that the number of British interceptions increased.

The weather was now an important factor. The German attacks on September 17 and 18 were minor and London was free from the Luftwaffe's attention by day although 170 bombers attacked on the night of the 17–18th and 268 on the next night. The German bombers were making these night raids unworried by either antiaircraft fire, which had grown in volume if not in accuracy, or by night fighters. Luftwaffe commanders, buoyed by the tall tales of London's destruction, were impressed by the possibility of a punishing offensive on the cheap. Yet the Germans were still able to register some notable successes by day.

On September 21 a single bomber, probably a Ju 88, penetrated to the Hawker factory at Weybridge which made Hurricanes. Bombing at 500 feet the German aircraft did some damage, although not enough to reduce production materially. The Supermarine Works near Southampton, from which most of the Spitfires came, was hit harder three days later. This time there were about twenty German planes. They damaged the factory itself only slightly but they hit an air-raid shelter killing or wounding about one hundred workers.

These attacks, which revealed that the Luftwaffe's dar-

ing was still in evidence, were followed by a more ambitious raid on the factory of the Bristol Aeroplane Company. This involved over fifty bombers from Luftflotte III
escorted by fighters. To draw off the British defenders
there was a second, smaller attack on Portland.

The defense was in difficulty from the outset. Three
squadrons were ordered into the air by No. 10 Group but
they were sent to Yeovil, where the Westland factory,
which also made aircraft, was located. When the Germans'
real target became obvious the British set off in pursuit.
But they were too late and the bombers reached their target with only one or two interceptions. The main assembly
works and other buildings were heavily and effectively
damaged by ninety tons of high explosive and twenty-four
oil bombs, more than 250 people were killed and wounded,
railways were blocked, and Filton airdrome's communications were cut. This was a sharp setback because production at the factory was cut for some weeks. The British
finally overhauled the raiders and shot down four German
planes. One more was picked off by antiaircraft guns. But
this was not much compensation for a successful raid of a
target deep in England.

Dowding at once moved a squadron to Filton airfield.
The move came none too soon. On September 27 the Germans turned up again, this time using Me 110 fighter-
bombers with an escort of fighters. The Hurricanes of 504
Squadron drove the raiders away from the target so that
their bombs fell in the suburbs of Bristol. Aircraft factories
were the main German targets by day during this stage of

the battle, an indication that the destruction of these all-important objectives could not be left to night bombing.

The Supermarine plant near Southampton was attacked on September 26 in another damaging raid. This time a force of about fifty bombers and fighter-bombers, heavily escorted, hit the plant with seventy tons of bombs. Production stopped. A Fighter Command without Spitfires would be like a boxer with only one fist. During the fighting that day four fighter squadrons from No. 10 and No. 11 Groups lost six planes while the Germans lost only two. The month came to an end with an attack by forty bombers on the Westland factory at Yeovil. This time the British got eight squadrons into the battle and the Germans failed to do any damage to the plant.

These attacks did a good deal of damage. They would have done more had it not been for the persistence and courage of the workers in the aircraft factories. More than thirty people were killed during the attack on the Supermarine Works and the other attacks also involved casualties. Yet the workers kept on the job. Often they had spent the night in shelters or in rescue work. Some were in the Home Guard. All were tired from weeks of work at high pressure by day and the wail of sirens and the crash of bombs by night. But when the bombers had gone and their factories blazed in ruins they returned to work on repairs and "to get cracking" on the job of sending aircraft to the RAF. There developed among them a curious kinship with the young men who flew the machines they made. The instinctive feeling that each was contributing

[220]

importantly to the defense of what they knew and loved was far more important than all the high-level appeals for "teamwork" between industry and the fighting forces.

Although these attacks on the aircraft industry had been effective, the Germans paid a very high price for their raids after September 15. From September 16 through September 30, the Luftwaffe lost a total of 238 fighters and bombers, the majority of them to Fighter Command by daylight. The German losses on the whole were heaviest when the target was London. On September 17, 27 and 30 the Luftwaffe attacked the capital with forces ranging from twenty-five to seventy-five aircraft. In each case the raiders were intercepted early and attacked heavily. Their losses for these three attacks on London by day were more than 120 planes against British losses of about sixty.

The success was due to Park's accurate assessment of the tactics necessary to halt raids on London made on the basis of his group's experiences during the fighting up to September 16. This was that the raiders could be successfully engaged only if there were a sufficient number of squadrons in the air to meet them in the initial stages and other squadrons at readiness on the ground which could be thrown into the battle at the critical point. This sufficed for attacks on London by bombers and fighters together. But Park also reviewed the group's arrangements for dealing with German fighters and fighter-bombers flying at high altitude. This produced the order, already mentioned, for patrols by pairs of Spitfire squadrons at great heights and instructions for avoiding German attack while the British formations were climbing to maximum altitude.

The total British losses in this period were 122 aircraft, all fighters. This was serious, but not as serious as it might have been a month earlier. Lord Beaverbrook's furious efforts to increase fighter production, which often involved methods highly displeasing to civil servants and other decorous fellows, were producing results. The low point in the supply of aircraft had been reached about September 7, when there were only 125 Spitfires and Hurricanes available. In the last three weeks of that month production overtook losses from all causes and the reserve figure began to rise. By the last week in October the reserves were higher than they had been since August.

The day battle was won by the pilots directed by Park, whose No. 11 Group from start to finish fought the great majority of the major actions, under the general command of Dowding, whose strategic and technical foresight had given Fighter Command the type of planes it needed, especially in the sphere of armament, for the battle it had to fight and had kept the command intact despite the urgent politico-military demands from France in May. Since ingratitude is not the exclusive prerogative of republics, the worldly will not be surprised to find that both officers were relieved of their commands in November and assigned to other less onerous and less important duties.

Military leaders seldom fight prolonged battles without suffering professional criticism. Park and Dowding were no exception. During the final phases of the day battle the former was criticized, especially by Air Vice-Marshal Trafford Leigh-Mallory, the commander of No. 12 Group, for his tactics. Leigh-Mallory's group had played an important part in the fighting on September 15 when five of its squadrons under the command of Squadron Leader Douglas Bader had flown down from Duxford to attack the German formations and reinforce No. 11 Group. Leigh-Mallory for some time had been experimenting with outsize formations of four or five or even seven squadrons fighting as a wing. His argument simply was that the wing was more powerful than the squadron or the two squadrons hunting as a pair favored by Park. Leigh-Mallory, then and later in the war, was a forceful debater. His arguments in 1944 against the plans for using the airborne forces on D day impressed, although they did not convince, that hardheaded soldier Lieutenant General Walter Bedell Smith, then General Eisenhower's Chief of Staff. But looking back to the debate of 1940 within the RAF there is a certain speciousness to his arguments. The wing from No. 12 Group had certainly been successful. But Leigh-Mallory had had time to mass his five squadrons, being farther from the initial point of contact with the Germans, whereas Park was fortunate if the warning gave him time to get two squadrons into position to intercept. Was not part of No. 12's success due to the fact that the German formations had already been savaged and broken up by No. 11 Group's squadron before the northern wing made contact? Leigh-Mallory's tactical panacea of the big wing was simple, so elementary that Park probably would have used it had he had time and had he been able to take the risk of leaving the vital sector stations without protective squadrons.

These considerations, however, did not weigh against the impression that Leigh-Mallory gave of a fresh mind supported by a driving personality available for the next stage of the war. So in November Park was assigned to command a flying training group and Leigh-Mallory took over at No. 11 Group. Later Park commanded the fighters in the long air battle in defense of Malta, displaying once again great resolution and judgment.

Dowding's eclipse also followed a period of criticism of his actions. His policy of maintaining only about half his available fighters in southern England on No. 11 Group's bases was attacked because it was said that, given the short range of the Me 109, the Luftwaffe's best fighter, the battle was sure to be fought over that area. Why not, the critics asked, concentrate a greater number of fighters in No. 11 Group to meet the blows that would surely fall there? Legitimately it was pointed out that the defeat suffered by Luftflotte V on August 15 had proved that without heavy escorting forces of Me 109's the Germans could not bomb effectively. Perhaps, but could Dowding, or any other commander so placed, be sure the Germans would *not* return to the north if the Luftwaffe learned that the fighter squadrons there had been moved south to reinforce No. 11 Group? Dowding could not be sure. Moreover, he feared that the sort of heavy reinforcement for the group envisaged by his critics would lead to over-crowding on the southern airfields and place an unwar-ranted burden on communications and control, which, after protracted German bombing, were not at peak efficiency.

On November 25, partly as a result of these and other criticisms and partly because he was worn out after months of terrible strain, Dowding left Fighter Command to be succeeded by Air Marshal Sholto Douglas. This officer was an advocate of big wing tactics who favored shooting down as many Germans as possible whenever they were found rather than emphasizing interception be-fore the enemy formations reached their targets. So Dow-ding left to go on a mission to the United States. With his Spitfires and Hurricanes, his pilots, professional and ama-teur, he had won a victory and created a legend. The com-mentator, twenty years later, cannot but conclude that he was shabbily treated.

Fighter Command was able to make these important changes because, as we have seen, the German offensive by day dwindled in October, compared to the attacks of the three preceding months. Still the German effort in daylight during October was enough to cost the Luftwaffe about 200 planes.

The focus of the German effort all through October, however, was London. The Luftwaffe's bomber forces had not been trained for night bombing, or indeed for long-range strategic raids, but they remained a formidable force, even after the punishment taken in the day battle.

There were over 700 bombers in Luftflotten II and III, each with a bomb load of more than a ton. Their bases were strung out from the Netherlands in the north to central France in the south. Consequently, it was unlikely that the capricious weather of Northwest Europe would immobilize the entire bombing force on any one night. The bombers also were aided by special transmitters which sent radio beams from the Continent across to England. German pilots flew on the beam until a different note in their earphones signaled that they had intersected another beam and were over the target. The system was known as "Knickbein," literally "crooked leg," and at the outset was of the greatest use to the Germans in locating and bombing important but isolated targets. When necessary, because of heavy antiaircraft defenses, the intersection could be made just short of the target, which then could be located by the concentration of searchlights and antiaircraft guns in action. "Knickbein" was not much needed for the raids on London. On a clear night, and especially after a heavy rain, the German pilots found the capital as easy to read as a map. The Germans also used their direction-finding beacons along the Channel coast to fix their positions and ensure accurate navigation. Finally, the British defenses, ground and air, remained rudimentary throughout the first weeks of the night attack. The Germans from Hitler down may have exaggerated the amount of damage the bombers were doing. It would be difficult to exaggerate the capital's unpreparedness to counter the bombings.

To the airmen night fighters rather than antiaircraft guns seemed the answer. The Blenheim, originally a bomber, was too slow for the job. The faster Beaufighter encountered a number of mechanical difficulties before it could be used extensively. But the chief problem was the unsuitability of radar equipment available to the night fighters at that time. The fighter had to get within three miles of the German bomber to make contact. After that it was a matter of the closest, most delicate cooperation between pilot and radar operator before the bomber could be brought to action. The use of GL radar sets, borrowed from the army, on the ground in conjunction with search-lights and antiaircraft guns, which later led to the system of Ground Control Interception, made some progress but there was a shortage of the type of set needed. The sug-gestion that more single-seater fighters, Hurricanes in this case, be assigned to night duties had little effect on the battle although it did exacerbate the differences between Dowding and the Air Staff. Fighter Command's chief be-lieved that the key to successful interception of German bombers at night lay in the use of radar in the air. Once again he was right although it was some months before he was proved so.

Airborne radar's chief difficulty was its limited range. The ground stations that had served Fighter Command so well during the day battle could probe over one hundred miles across the Channel into Europe to pick up German aircraft. The original airborne sets did well if they could "sight" a German plane at three miles. A later version, which was tested in August, had a longer range and appeared to be less susceptible to the rigors of service in fighter aircraft. But production was slow and the type of fighter necessary unavailable at the time.

During this period the British tried a variety of remedies. One favorite was PAC (Parachute and Cable), a device which fired rockets to a height of just over 500 feet. The rockets were attached to light steel cables carrying parachutes. The parachutes opened and the dangling cables were supposed to form a barrier to the German bombers. Another version was the double-parachute link, a steel cable joining two parachutes. "Mutton" was a weapon made of 2,000 feet of piano wire, a parachute, and a bomb. The parachute was at the top, the piano wire in the middle and the bomb at the end. The idea was that a number of these would be suspended before an approaching German formation—provided, of course, that it could be located—and the bombers would obligingly fly into the wire. This would bring the bomb up to explode next to his aircraft and, as the RAF said, "Good-by Herman." Theory was better than practice. These attempts to defeat an enemy who had the limitless space of the night sky in which to approach his targets sound highly comic today. They were not so comic then when each night brought another attack on London and each dawn more destruction and more casualties. The RAF and the government would rightly have been considered lacking in enterprise had they not explored every suggestion that offered even a shadow of relief for London.

[228]

The night fighters, which eventually proved the most reliable killers of German bombers, did not become really effective until the spring of 1941, a period outside the scope of this record. By then the long, terrible winter was ended.

The German bombing that had begun on September 7 was unrelenting. Unusually bad weather forced a halt on the night of November 3–4 but the attacks were resumed the next night. The German records report that 8,300 tons of high explosive were dropped on London during October and the first half of November.

London's size was so great that the physical damage done by the Germans never measured up to the claims made by the Luftwaffe. The bombing was termed "indiscriminate" by the British at the time but the fact remains that an enormous amount of damage was done to the type of targets whose destruction fitted the German aim of making life unbearably difficult for the people of the city. This was true of railways, docks, and the suburban rail services on which hundreds of thousands of Londoners depended for transport to and from their work.

The casualties were not so great as had been anticipated before the war. The government had ordered that 120,000 beds should be reserved in the hospitals for casualties of the bombing. During October, the height of the Blitz, only 6,343 people were admitted to hospital. Yet the scale of the attacks can be measured by the raid of October 15 made by about 400 bombers. Train service was halted at five main stations. Traffic at four others was cut by more than two thirds. The city's underground railway system was cut at five places. Roads were blocked throughout the city and a reservoir, three gasworks, two power stations, and three important docks were hit. There were 900 fires in London that night. Over 400 people were killed and more than 800 badly wounded.

Goering believed, or at least told his pilots, that their attacks on "the head of the British Empire, the city of London with its eight and one half million inhabitants, have reduced the British plutocracy to fear and terror." It was about this time that Churchill, making his way across London at the height of an attack, heard a Home Guard sing out, "It's a grand life, if you don't weaken." The Londoners in October and November showed little signs of weakening. For the human animal is marvelously adaptable.

In many cases the substitution of a new shelter routine enabled ordinary men and women to live a life unthinkable a few months earlier: A quick supper at home, if the home still stood, or a meal in the shelter cooked at someone else's home and brought underground before the man returned from work. Gossip in the evening with old neighbors and new acquaintances met in the shelter. A night's sleep, uneasy perhaps because of the bombs and guns, but probably a better sleep than most people got outside the shelters. Then, in the morning, the man off to work and the daily routine beginning again. At the outset many of the shelters were bare. Heat and light were easy to arrange. Bunks came later and, as Fitz Gibbon has reported,

"a surprising amount of opposition was met from the shel-
terers themselves." Bunks, you see, occupied space and
some people might have to leave the shelter. And in the
East End folk by now accustomed to sleeping on the floor
refused to sleep in bunks. Could routine go much further?

Life in the shelters was hard and graceless. The phrase
" 'Tisn't so bad, y'know," which one heard at the time was
a terrible indictment of the living conditions of many
Londoners. At first when I heard it I was willing to accept
it as yet another example of that obstinate cheerfulness
under stress encountered so often during the war. But
Evelyn Montague pointed out that for many of those in
the shelters it really wasn't so bad; that the rat-infested,
lousy quarters they had known before the Blitz were, in
some respects, worse than their present quarters in the
shelters. The complaint heard most often was not of the
living conditions but of the absence of entertainment. "I
miss the flicks." Despite the horrendous tales, some of
them true, about scores of people killed when bombs fell
in crowded movie houses, the movies remained the chief
avenue of escape from the Blitz.

"Gran was in the country, evacuated and all," a mother
told me one night in Stepney. "Couldn't stand it. No flicks,
she said, no nothing. Dull it was." So they stayed by the
sordid streets they knew. In many cases entertainment was
organized by the shelter dwellers themselves. Amateur
theatricals, that passion of the middle class, was a bit beyond them. But shelters rang to the rousing chorus of

"Knees Up, Mother Brown" and other Cockney favorites. There was always someone in the shelter who could play a musical instrument. There were innumerable games of cards. The London County Council took a hand. Paperback books were distributed and classes were organized; those dealing with current affairs were not much of a success. Earnest people from the Council for the Encouragement of Music and the Arts invaded the shelters with gramophones and classical records.

In 1945 enthusiastic Labour party members claimed that the foundation of their party's great victory in the General Election that year was laid in the shelters of London. There may be some truth in this. But a great many of the men and women in the shelters were Labour voters before they went underground. Their experiences underground may have strengthened their resolve that "them," the rich, the governing class, would have their comeuppance when the war was over. But I do not remember hearing politics talked at great length. People were willing enough to talk about their lives or about the war generally. There was a strong desire for revenge on the Germans, sometimes softened by humanity. "If they can get them what's up there bombing us, all right," a woman said one night. "But I wouldn't want nobody to have to go through what me and Jim has, them Germans at home, I mean."

On the whole they were not people of great imagination. Mercifully the picture seen by those with greater imagination—and information—was hidden from them.

[232]

About 5,000 people were killed in London during the month of October and every morning brought a new report of railroad lines blocked or temporarily destroyed, public utilities put out of action, factories damaged. "Our outlook at this time was that London, except for its strong modern buildings, would be gradually and soon reduced to a rubble-heap," wrote Churchill. But the people against whose will to endure the whole offensive was being directed lived on, cheered by small things, the report of a bomber brought down by the guns or a bottle of gin rescued from a blazing pub; "Cor, didn't 'alf 'ave a party on that," the air-raid warden, who had mistaken a falling land mine for a parachutist and who, incredibly, had lived to tell about it.

The Battle of London was the most advertised part of the greater Battle of Britain, which included, in addition to the great air battles by day, the bombing of industrial cities in the provinces. After the war Goering was certain that he had convinced Hitler to allow the Luftwaffe to make these attacks because they "would be much more valuable. I argued that it was no use to us to have another hundred houses go up in flames. I wished for attacks on the aircraft plants in the south of England and around Coventry, the shipping yards, Glasgow, Birmingham and the ports. I told the Fuehrer again and again that inasmuch as I knew the British people as well as I did my own, we should never force them to their knees by bombing London."

Skeptics may question this last statement. Goering's

character was such that he was probably more moved by the absence of any overwhelming success by the Luftwaffe than by any sudden insight into British character. The Luftwaffe had lost the daylight battle although Goering was careful to maintain the fiction that it had won; something that was increasingly difficult to do under the cold eyes of the professionals. What he wanted now for himself and his service was something big, something he could brag about at court. He got it.

Luftflotten II and III had been bombing London about as they pleased. They were naturally suffering some losses but the majority of these were the result of crashes on landing after the return flight rather than from British defense activities. The pilots knew now that the RAF had night fighters in the air, they even occasionally saw them, and very occasionally were engaged by one. But the strain imposed by the presence of fighters and the greatly augmented antiaircraft barrage may have had something to do with these crashes. The German aircrews also knew or guessed that the British were jamming the beams whereon "Knickbein" operated or even deflecting them away from targets. This did not make much difference to the bombing of London but it made the bombing of isolated industrial targets more difficult. But German science had found an answer to the British tactics of "bending the beam" in the form of devices that would enable the Luftwaffe to reach and attack individual industrial targets. It offered the Luftwaffe X Apparatus and Y Apparatus, which, although complicated and necessitating the installation of new receiving sets to pick up the beams or to receive, in the case of Y Apparatus, messages from a German controller who would order the release of bombs when, according to his calculations, the bomber was over the target. British intelligence services were aware of the imminence of heavy attacks on industrial cities by the middle of November although they did not know the identity of the cities or the details of the new location systems that were to guide the bombers.

The first and probably the most destructive attack was that on Coventry on the night of November 14. The Germans called the operation "Moonlight Sonata." British propaganda at the time pictured the raid as a deliberate attempt to destroy a city and kill its people. Actually the bomber formations, or Kampfgruppen, were assigned to important industrial targets like the Standard Motor Company, the Coventry Radiator and Press Company, the British Piston Ring Company, the Daimler Motor Works, and the Alvis Aeroengine factory. They were to use the first of the new German control systems—X Geraet or X Apparatus. Under this system the bomber flew along a thin beam in the center of a broader beam. This approach beam was intersected by three beams closer to the objective. The first was a general warning to prepare for the attack. The second was a preliminary signal for attack. The third was the final signal which meant that the bomber was only a short distance from its target.

The night was bright, cold and moonlit. The first

bombers arrived at about 8:15 P.M. They were from Kampfgruppe 100, which made a specialty of blind bombing against precision targets. This group's function was similar to that of the Pathfinders of the RAF's Bomber Command later in the war; they found the target and set it afire with incendiary bombs. The remainder of the force bombed on the fires. These took a number of other routes to the target. All told, the Germans used 437 planes. By the time the last bomber had droned eastward at about six o'clock the next morning the Luftwaffe had dropped fifty-six tons of incendiary bombs, 127 parachute mines, or, as they were then called, land mines, and 394 tons of high-explosive bombs. Coventry was in ruins.

Kampfgruppe 100 had been very successful. The fires it kindled took hold and the successive formations of German bombers, aided by the bright moonlight, had no trouble locating their targets. Compared to London, Coventry was a small target and one got the impression of total destruction that was absent from the worst raids on the capital. The German bombs knocked out the telephone system and damaged the water mains early in the attack, impeding rescue work and reducing the effectiveness of the fire services. The city seemed to be ablaze. There was no refuge from the heat or from the intolerable crackling and crashing of burning and falling buildings. Without water and without communication, the civil defense workers fought as soldiers fight in the midst of an overwhelming enemy attack, doing what they could, where they could, with what they had at hand to save lives and property on the ground. They could do nothing to halt the parade of bombers over the city.

The bombs blocked the railway lines to Birmingham, Leamington, Rugby and Nuneaton. They severely damaged twenty-one important factories or industrial plants, twelve of which were directly concerned with the production of RAF planes. The damage done to power and telephone lines and to water and gas mains automatically halted work in nine plants that had escaped serious damage. Thousands of homes were blown to bits or burned to the ground. Dozens of streets were closed by rubble. Between four and five hundred small shops were either destroyed or put out of business. It was estimated that about 550 people were killed and another 850 seriously injured. Time after time rescue teams made up of men who had been working at great speed and in intense heat for hours plunged down blazing streets and often into burning houses to carry men and women, already wounded, to safety.

The reactions of the German and British governments to this smashing blow offer an interesting study in national character. The Luftwaffe High Command judged that Coventry and its industry had been knocked out and the next night it sent only sixteen bombers to the city. The weather was bad and only seven or eight reached the city, where they did little to add to the damage done twenty-four hours previously. This reflected the familiar German error of exaggerating the extent of their success. Had the Luftwaffe repeated the raid of the previous night on the night of November 15–16 or even the succeeding night, Coventry might have been removed from British industrial calculations for about a year. But it did not and therefore gave Coventry the opportunity to show how remarkably quickly an industrial population and an industrial city can recover.

The first problem was to quell the fires. The firemen worked through that grisly day and by nightfall on the 15th the fires were under control although enough of them burned to guide German bombers should they return in force. Troops brought in from nearby camps cleared paths through the rubble while battered, smoking streets were kept clear by the police of all but essential traffic. The railway lines presented a worse problem. By working round the clock the British got all lines but the one to Nuneaton open by the night of November 18. Bomb-disposal squads were brought in to deal with the large number of unexploded bombs in the city. The highways serving the city were in fairly good shape. On the night of November 16 the authorities arranged to take 10,000 people out of the city's center. Only 300 of them were willing to go. Such was the spirit of the people. Remember, they all expected another raid, and knew that the antiaircraft guns and the night fighters offered little protection. But they stayed where they were.

Transport was organized to take homeless workers from shelter found outside the city to their plants when these returned to operation. Half the work force at the Standard Motor Company was on hand on the morning of the 16th and one factory manager found men who had been up throughout the night doing rescue work "pitching in to get things cleared up."

Neither the RAF nor the antiaircraft gunners had been able to do much during the raid. The night fighters flew 125 sorties along the approaches to the city but only two of them got close enough to German raiders to open fire. The gunners claimed one plane shot down at Loughborough and at Birmingham some of them saw another exploded in the air.

Now committed to an offensive against industrial cities, the Luftwaffe picked out Southampton, where the dreaded Spitfires were made, on November 17. Then on the nights of November 19, 20 and 22 they hammered Birmingham, another important industrial target, with a total of 762 tons of high explosive and 1,563 incendiary canisters. The Luftwaffe got 677 bombers over the target during the three nights. On the 23rd the Germans returned to Southampton. From that point onward throughout the remainder of November and December the Luftwaffe ranged over southern and western England and the Midlands. Southampton was hit twice, on November 30 and December 1, Birmingham again on the 11th. Then it was Sheffield's turn. A big force, 336 aircraft, attacked the city on the night of December 12, dropping 355 tons of high explosive and 457 incendiary canisters. The Liverpool-Birkenhead area was subjected to two heavy attacks on December 20 and 21, involving a total of 504 bombers; 413 tons of high explosive and 1,701 canisters of incendiaries. Manchester was next, just before Christmas. Then after a series of relatively quiet nights London was visited with the great fire raid on December 29. This was a Sunday night. Although the Germans did not know it, their raid, which by their standards was not a heavy one, using only 127 tons of high explosive and 613 canisters of incendiaries, was made under favorable circumstances. For the main weight of the attack fell on the City, the financial and commercial center of the capital, an area full of old buildings most of them securely locked against burglars and insufficiently guarded by fire watchers. The incendiary bombs sprayed from the canisters were not difficult to deal with if they could be located when they first fell. Once they got a fire going the dry old buildings and a brisk wind did the rest.

The attempts to fight the series of enormous fires that soon took hold were hampered by a shortage of water. High-explosive bombs smashed one of the principal mains. The emergency water tanks soon ran dry. The Thames was so low that the pumps could make little use of its water. Firemen stood in the face of the greatest fire since the great fire of London of 1666 in Stuart times and saw the streams from the nozzles dwindle to trickles. The Germans bombed for two hours. When they departed there were over 1,400 fires, six of them classed as "conflagrations," the highest category, most of them in the City but others in neighboring boroughs. The largest of these, covering half a square mile, swept through Moorgate, Aldersgate Street, Cannon Street and Old Street leaving an empty area where the scars are still visible today, twenty years later. The angry flames lit the sky and against this orange-red background rose the great dome of St. Paul's.

Again, as in Coventry, the rescue workers performed prodigies of valor. They guided people out of shelters that were either in the path of the fire or underneath buildings already ablaze. They clambered out onto the roofs of buildings to pitch incendiaries into the streets. They made vain, brave attempts to halt the march of the flames with buckets of water. All this in the midst of a roaring inferno that blistered their faces and sent showers of sparks driving into their eyes and noses and mouths. Sixteen of the 163 people killed were firemen.

The fires closed the General Post Office, the Central Telegraph office, and three telephone exchanges. Five railway stations and sixteen underground stations were out of action the next morning. Eight of Sir Christopher Wren's churches perished. The City of London, so long the citadel of Britain's financial power, lay smoldering and blackened in the dawn. But St. Paul's, saved by its fire watchers, survived. One incendiary fell on the dome perilously close to the old timbers between the dome's outer and inner shells. It seemed a matter of moments to the anxious watchers before the incendiary would set the whole dome ablaze. Suddenly the bomb fell off the dome and was extinguished.

Thus in flame and smoke, in death and destruction, the year came to its end. There was now hardly a major city or town in England from Liverpool and Manchester south that had escaped attack. The civil defense services had been strained to the utmost. The industrial economy had been gravely damaged and communications impeded. The attacks were to continue on into the new year and extend westward to Wales and northward to Glasgow, the Clyde and the Tyne. But when the lights of the first day of 1941 fell across Berlin the masters of the Third Reich were no longer concentrating on Britain and its cities. They were thinking of Russia. As far as Hitler was concerned, the war in Europe was won. On January 8 and 9 he summoned his commanders in chief and his ministers to the Berghof and at the end of the meeting the audience was given a summary of the Fuehrer's thinking.

"I am firmly convinced that the situation in Europe can no longer developed unfavorably for Germany even if we should lose the whole of North Africa. Our position is so firmly established in Europe that the outcome cannot possibly be to our disadvantage. The invasion of Britain is not feasible unless she is crippled to a considerable degree, and Germany has complete air superiority. The success of an invasion must be completely assured, otherwise it would be a crime to attempt it. The British can hope to win the war only by beating us on the Continent. I am convinced that this is impossible. Attacks on Britain must be concentrated on supplies and the armament industry. Terror raids by the Luftwaffe have small value and accomplish little; the supplies and the ships bringing them must be destroyed. Combined assaults by the Luftwaffe and the navy on imports might lead to a victory as early as July or August. Even today I am still ready to negotiate peace with Britain. However, Britain's present leaders will not consider such a peace."

So in January Hitler turned his back on Britain. The bombing and the U-boat warfare would continue. But the great objective, the conquest of Britain by invasion, had been abandoned and, although Hitler still clung to his illusion that the British could be bombed or starved into submission, few of his military advisers agreed. So the Battle for Britain ended.

Chapter XI

Gash'd with honourable scars,
  Low in Glory's lap they lie,
Though they fell, they fell like stars,
  Streaming splendour through the sky.

—JAMES MONTGOMERY, "Battle of Alexandria"

The Battle of Britain was the culmination of the long duel between the United Kingdom and Germany that had begun in the naval rivalry of the nineties and had continued intermittently for fifty years thereafter. Twice the two powers had been the leaders of contending coalitions. The period between the fall of France in June, 1940, and the end of that year was, however, the only one in which the two nations faced each other alone. The British were alone by force of circumstance. One by one their allies had been overrun by the legions of the Third Reich. The Empire was far away, unprepared for war, and its members had their own strategic preoccupations. The Germans, although they could now draw upon the industrial resources of Western Europe, fought Britain without the military help of Italy. Perhaps encumbrance would be a better word than help. After 1940 the war developed into a true world war, a conflict of coalitions and alliances. But for those five and one half months it was a naked trial of strength between the two great European powers that had emerged from the Victorian age.

The word "battle" was used loosely during the Second World War. It became the fashion to describe prolonged military operations as "battles" instead of campaigns. However, since the German objective from start to finish in 1940 was the defeat of Britain and because this was the only military objective sought by the German government and its military command between June and December, the series of operations by day and night can be considered together as the Battle of Britain.

This battle, as our account shows, passed through three stages. They are not distinct. Often they overlapped. But the distinction is clearer now than it was in the heat of the fighting.

The first and most important stage was the battle in the air by day. This is what is usually termed the "Battle of Britain." The second stage was the bombing of London by night, which Londoners called "the Blitz" and the rest of the world called the Battle of London. The third, least well-known stage was the bombing, again by night, of Britain's industrial cities. The night attacks on London began before the day battle had ended. The bombing of the provincial cities started while London was still under attack and, although at times these other attacks lightened the burden of the Londoners, the Luftwaffe always returned to the capital. In fact the last great German attack in the West by manned aircraft for the whole of the war was the very heavy raid on London on the night of May 10–11, 1941.

The day battle must be considered the most important stage of the German offensive against Britain because upon its outcome hung the fate of Operation "Sea Lion." The best chance of German victory seemed then to be through successful invasion of the British Isles. Today, even though we know more about the strengths and weaknesses of both sides, this still appears true. But although when the second stage of the battle began with the bombing of London on September 7 invasion had been postponed, the Germans were still striving by other means to accomplish the subjugation of Britain. This was true, too, of the third stage. Hitler, as Winston Churchill perceived in June, knew "that he will have to break us in this island or lose the war." From the middle of June onward every German action from the strafing of a fishing boat to the massive raid on Coventry was directed toward that end. These operations failed. The Germans did not break the British. On the contrary, they were defeated decisively in the day battle and all their efforts in the bombings of London and the industrial cities did not suffice to cripple the economy of the kingdom or sap the resolution of its people.

We have all read this time and time again. We know the consequences that flowed from those five and one-half months of battle. But the true significance of the Battle of Britain is best understood if we alter history, if we suppose for a moment that the Germans had won, either through successful invasion or through the collapse of British resistance under the bombs, and an abject surrender. What would have been the consequences then?

Hitler would have gorged upon British industry, for the terms of peace dictated to the United Kingdom would have been onerous indeed. Those few who were foolish enough in 1940 to talk of a patched-up peace with the Germans should have read the Treaty of Brest-Litovsk dictated by the Germans to the Soviet Union. The Versailles "Diktat," as the Nazis called it, was mild in comparison. Having fattened the Wehrmacht on the output of British industry and agriculture, the German dictator would then have turned east. Since Britain was defeated and occupied, it would not have been necessary to leave Luftflotte III in Western Europe, as in reality he did. Nor, it is reasonable to assume, would large numbers of troops have been required to maintain the subjugation of the occupied nations. Resistance to occupation flourishes when there is hope, however small, of liberation. The defeat of Britain would have been the defeat of hope.

The Fuehrer's drive to the east would not have been delayed, as was the actual invasion of the Soviet Union, by the necessity of quelling the sudden, brief upsurge of Yugoslav resistance or of smashing the allied British and Greek forces in Greece; operations that cost the Germans precious weeks of good campaigning weather. The attack on the Soviet Union in 1941 would have begun in May rather than in June. The Germans would have been stronger both in the air and on the ground. They came very close to defeating the Russians in the field in the late summer and early autumn of 1941 as it was. How would the Russians have fared had the Germans had just that little bit more, those extra squadrons of bombers, that additional army corps?

Field Marshal Gerd von Rundstedt had no illusions. He told some Russian officers in 1945 that, had the Luftwaffe won the Battle of Britain in 1940, Germany would have defeated the Soviet Union the next year. They had come to ask his view on the decisive battle of the war, thinking, of course, that he would name Stalingrad. When, his old eyes cold, his face stiff and proud, von Rundstedt told them "the Battle of Britain," they folded their notebooks and went away.

Under the first agonizing shock of the fall of France those Britons in high places who thought their island could not be defended against the Germans believed that, in Churchill's words used in a more bellicose context, "in God's good time, the new world, with all its power and might" would step forth "to the rescue and the liberation of the old." Although the British won the battle, we should not overlook the fact that in those hours a great many men, able, competent and courageous, believed that it might come to this. Were their hopes justified?

The state of public opinion in the United States in 1940 was not encouraging. The state of the armed forces was downright discouraging. The conquest of Britain would have been a paralyzing shock. The most likely reactions would not have been a crusade for the liberation of Europe but a withdrawal into what was later termed "Fortress America," leaving the world to the domination of the Germans, the Japanese and the Italians. Our time would have come. But it would have come when the Germans and their allies chose. Such would have been the consequences of a British defeat in 1940.

The air battle by day was the decisive part of the Battle of Britain because the defeat of the Luftwaffe was the principal, although not the only, factor in dissuading the Germans from the invasion of Britain, which was at once the most certain and most costly way of conquering the islanders. But this British victory within a victory had other results of great importance to the future course of the war. One of the most interesting of these was the psychological impact upon the German armed forces. Of these the Luftwaffe alternately was considered as the favorite son or a suspicious interloper. Reborn under the Nazis, the German air force was more heavily flavored by the ideology of national socialism than either of the two senior services. In Reichsmarschall Goering, its chief, the Luftwaffe had an unrivaled advocate at the court of King Adolf. In the first campaigns of the war the army and navy had suffered checks here and there. The *Graf Spee* had been burned and scuttled off Montevideo. H.M.S. *Warspite* had pounded a flotilla of German destroyers into smoldering hulks at Narvik. The British Expeditionary Force had given as good as it got at Louvain, had counter-attacked at Arras with initial success, and at Calais had held for four days a position the Germans thought they would take in as many hours. These were demerits on the German army's record.

But the Luftwaffe, ah, the Luftwaffe was invincible. Poles, Norwegians, Belgians and French had all been swept from the skies. Only the English remained. Its failure to sweep the RAF from the skies—for even Goering had to recognize failure if not defeat—ended the legend of invincibility of the Luftwaffe. In 1944, when the Allies returned to France, I asked French and Belgians when they began to doubt a German victory. Invariably they set the date as late 1940 when, working in the fields, they would look up and see high above them British fighter formations. They knew then that despite all they heard and read that the British had won the battle in the air. It is perhaps relevant that at about this time the first stirrings of organized resistance to the Germans became apparent in Northwest Europe.

But the victory in the day battle did more than smash the legend of the Luftwaffe's invincibility and provide hope for the conquered. It also demonstrated that the Germans had no monopoly on the advanced techniques of modern war. During the fighting in France important people all over the world became mesmerized by the speed and efficiency with which the Germans won their victories. Here was a war machine perfectly tooled, precise; no fumbling, no uncertainties. Actually there had been errors in the field and moments of buck fever in the High Command, as General Heinz Guderian's account recalls, but these were obscured by German propaganda. In Washing-

ton, in Moscow, in a dozen other capitals, me
at the German war machine, and the foolisl
that only totalitarianism could produce forc
cally perfect. France, poor, old bumbling France ..
love for those three beautiful sisters, Liberté, Egalité,
Fraternité, had gone under. The Third Republic with its
follies and triumphs, its great men and knaves, its sweet-
ness of life had gone under; no match for those ruthlessly
efficient Prussians. Now it was England's turn. How could
the intensely conservative islanders hold the Germans? In
Washington many wished the British well publicly. Privately they considered it was only a question of time.

Slowly it became apparent that a democracy out of all
its fumbling, its long-drawn raucous debates, its absurd
reverence for the secret ballot could match the totali-
tarians. The first, the greatest technical surprise of the
Battle of Britain, the mechanical achievement that probably did more than anything else to compensate the RAF
for its numerical inferiority was radar; a device that originated in the slumbering, peaceful Britain of the prewar
years when the eyes of Europe and of half the world were
watching the steel-tipped columns of Hitler's new army.
Despite its early failings, despite its undependable moments, radar remained the eyes of the RAF. Here, incredibly, was a marvelous British device which the Germans wished they had. Here was a technical achievement
for democracy.

Those foolish, pleasure-loving plutocrats on their island
also developed, as the battle wore on, other devices that

helped frustrate the German offensive. Casual, rather diffident men—how different from the precise, confident scientists of the new Germany—emerged from old universities to suggest they "rather thought they had something that might make a mess of Knickbein." Anyhow, they would tell the Air Council and the lowering, impatient Churchill, they would play about with it and let them all know. In that war, which Churchill has called "the Wizards' War," these seemingly ineffectual fellows were the masters until the end.

At the end of the battle for France the German air force and its machines were the wonder and envy of the military world. Once again a surprise. The British had built a couples of planes, the Spitfire and the Hurricane, and a man named Dowding, an air officer who unaccountably thought little of parades and reviews, had armed them with eight machine guns and trained their pilots to extract every advantage that lay in their extreme maneuverability. Yes, it appeared that a democracy could produce technical surprises to confound the Germans and their efficient, totalitarian system. It was not decisive. But it was hopeful.

During the early summer it was also noticeable that a democracy, when pushed, could act with ruthlessness too. The decision to withhold British fighters from France was a hard one to take. But it was taken. So was the decision to attack the French fleet at Mers-el-Kebir. But it was taken. Obviously the British had the bit between their teeth. There were naturally elderly diplomats in Berlin who could have told Hitler that the British, once driven to war, a calamity they invariably try to avert by all sorts of policies, some of them rather discreditable, would prove the most ruthless and implacable of all his foes. But in a totalitarian state no one offers advice of this sort to the leader once he has made up his mind that the intended enemy is cowardly because he hesitates, weak because he scorns might.

The twin legends of Germans invincibility in the air and matchless technical superiority had been exploded. But other legends grew out of the battle and some of these persist to this day. Of these the most persistent is that the day battle was a relatively easy victory and that Fighter Command of the RAF ended the battle stronger than it was at the outset. The origin of this legend, I believe, is the greatly exaggerated claims of German losses put out by the Air Ministry during the battle and corrected when the Luftwaffe's records became available after the war. These figures, issued night after night to a public which slowly was recognizing that Fighter Command stood between it and even greater peril, gave a false picture of staggering German losses in the day battle. When the correct figures were disclosed, the people of Britain paid less attention. Their minds were on other things. The battle had been fought a long time ago, it seemed, and "we won easily, knocked the Jerries for six." During the war the Air Ministry claimed that between July 10 and October 31, 1940, a total of 2,698 German planes had been destroyed. Actually the Germans lost 1,733. The Luftwaffe's claims were even more exaggerated. The German

High Command's figures for the period were 3,058 British planes destroyed. In fact the RAF lost 915 aircraft. The British counted an even graver loss in the death of about 415 pilots through enemy action. These young men, the flower of the professional, prewar air force, could never be replaced. Aside from the fact that the German losses were exaggerated by just under one thousand, the story of the fighting shows exactly how close the whole thing was. It will suffice to cite only one example. On September 15, the climax of the battle, all the British squadrons available were committed to action at the moment of maximum German pressure. There was nothing left. The game was on the table.

Reflection on the day battle shows that twice Goering picked up and tried the keys to victory. But each time, possibly because the lock did not click immediately, he discarded the key and tried another. Early in August the German attacks on the stations in the British radar system, the eyes of the RAF, were proceeding successfully. Then Goering and the High Command discontinued the attacks. What would have happened had the raids continued? Fighter Command in August was intercepting German formations with only seconds to spare. Without radar, depending only on the Observer Corps, which could not operate, of course, until the Germans were over England, the number of interceptions undoubtedly would have fallen and the number of unopposed attacks on key targets risen.

Then in late August and early September the Luftwaffe

began and nourished a series of successful raids on the sector stations. Effective attacks on the radar stations would have blinded Fighter Command. Heavy damage to the sector stations would have paralyzed it. Veterans of the battle on the British side regard the German diversions away from the radar stations and sector stations as the first two turning points in the conflict. And why did Goering turn from the sector stations? Because he could not stick to the steady, methodical, unspectacular but immensely important task of eliminating the sector stations when there was the opportunity to show off the Luftwaffe as a force capable of hammering London into submission. All the calculations that would have weighed in the mind of a veteran air officer—and we often forget that Goering was a veteran air officer—apparently were discarded. The long flight into London. The certainty that the RAF would throw all its reserves into the defense of the capital. These did not count. Here was a showy, easy victory. Besides, everyone knew that the British were beaten. On to London. It was his biggest mistake; one of the worst made by the Germans in the war.

The gravity of the mistake is obvious. It has the additional merit of throwing light on the follies of totalitarianism at war. A professional airman who erred to this extent should have been axed by his government. You cannot ax a Reichsmarschall in the middle of a war even if you are Adolf Hitler. For you, even you, the Fuehrer, are the prisoner of that splendid propaganda so cleverly contrived by Dr. Goebbels. The Luftwaffe is winning, London is being destroyed, and the RAF is no longer a factor in the battle. Goering remains to make other mistakes and the tendency of the regime to lay grandiose plans on the basis of subjective reasoning and false information continues unchecked.

Some of the blame for Goering's errors must be laid to the German intelligence services. The deference paid to the supposedly omniscient officers of the Abwehr during the war seems incredible in the light of what we now know of its operations. But in those days it was an article of faith that not only were the ears of the enemy everywhere but they were damnably acute. Almost any group could produce one person who knew someone who had heard Lord Haw Haw report that the town clock at Much Haddam was broken. "And do you know, old chap, when they checked on it they found the clock was broken. Uncanny, isn't it? Those devils must be everywhere." "They" weren't everywhere. Indeed, on the German side the gathering of intelligence about the beleaguered island and the interpretation of such intelligence as was received were of a low standard.

It might be thought, for instance, that in the months before the war the location of British fighter airfields in southern England would be the prime objective of German agents. God knows, they were not hard to find. But when the battle began the Luftwaffe spent a good deal of time and wasted a good many tons of bombs hammering away at bases that had almost nothing to do with the operations of its archenemy, Fighter Command. This was just as well. For when the Germans finally did locate the airfields and the sector stations, largely because some of the Luftwaffe pilots used their eyes and common sense, they gave them a fearful beating.

The absence of accurate German intelligence is one of the reasons for thinking that British resistance to invasion would have come as a shock to the Germans. They were ludicrously wrong about the British order of battle. Sir Anthony Eden, then Secretary of State for War, has recalled that after Dunkirk there was only one division, the 2nd Canadian Infantry Division, up to strength and fully equipped in the British Isles and that for many weeks thereafter the ground forces were in the throes of reorganization, very short of antitank guns and all other forms of artillery, and striving to train the intake of new soldiers. This chaotic condition which, if known to the German High Command, might have induced them to chance a snap invasion, was hidden from those clever devils of the Abwehr.

Toward the end of August, when the British army was still in such a state that professionals silently thanked the Deity for the presence of the RAF and the Royal Navy, the official German estimate of British ground strength was thirty-four and one-half divisions, twenty-two of which were rated as "completely operational." At the time the British Home Forces had twenty-nine divisions, about seven of which approached the German divisions in firepower. There can be little doubt that throughout those months of stress the Abwehr was of the greatest help to the

British cause. Indeed, the story that Admiral Canaris, its head, was a secret sympathizer with the British cause, or even a British agent, probably originated in these laughably inaccurate estimates and in the failure of his organization to provide the Luftwaffe with even the most rudimentary information.

Deprived of accurate information about the British forces and their location, the Germans also suffered from another handicap intrinsic in all authoritarian states. This is the tendency to lie in order to curry favor with the man on the next higher rung of the ladder.

Goering was told on most occasions what he wanted to hear. He told his colleagues in the other services what he wanted them to hear. They all told Hitler what they thought he wanted to hear and what would shed the brightest light upon their own efforts. In such an atmosphere, objective reasoning is impossible. By the end of the war this prevarication at the top had pervaded all the forces. Only a few stubborn old generals clung to the truth. And how much did their cautious objections weigh against the confident dreams of the Nazis? Not an ounce. Lies blinded the Germans almost as much as the loss of radar would have blinded the British.

The reader may conclude at this point that the Battle of Britain was lost by the Germans rather than won by the British. In retrospect it is always easier to detect the errors on the side of the losers than it is to point out those decisions which led to victory. To this day there are grave differences among the experts over exactly why the Battle of the Marne, the decisive battle of World War I, was won, although there is complete agreement that the Germans lost it. So it is with the Battle of Britain. Let me list a few of the reasons why the British won it.

First, technical superiority that was never approached by the Germans. The Luftwaffe came close to knocking out the radar system. But it never came close to constructing a corresponding system. The German technical advances were directed toward making bombing more accurate, and in the end all of these were frustrated by the British.

Second, the qualitative superiority of Fighter Command. Individually there was little to choose between the regular RAF and Luftwaffe pilots in courage or morale, although the fact that they were fighting over and for their homeland undoubtedly strengthened the resolution of the British airmen. The Luftwaffe, however, had received in the two years before the Battle of Britain a large number of new pilots and other airmen who, by British standards, were somewhat sketchily trained. The over-all quality of its bomber crews suffered as a result. Midway through the battle the Luftwaffe High Command, increasingly concerned by the losses of trained officers, ordered that no bomber henceforth should carry more than a single officer on an operational mission. Fighter Command, however, had not been flooded by new pilots. Far from it! It began the battle therefore with a higher percentage of seasoned professional pilots.

The technical training of the British fighter pilots seems

to have been a shade better than that of their German adversaries. Fighter Command was smaller but it was more attuned to the requirements of independent air operations, more professional, and the majority of its pilots had been better trained. Once more, as in 1914, an army of mercenaries "saved the sum of things for pay."

Third, as the battle progressed Park and Dowding exhibited a flexibility in tactics and a resolution in strategy that the Germans lacked. The reader will have seen that No. 11 Group was sometimes surprised by new German tactics. But it was almost never surprised and off balance for more than a few hours. Park fought the entire battle on the defensive. In the nature of things no other course was open. But he showed marvelous adaptability in meeting the changes in German tactics. Intermittently in the battle the Germans would grasp the initiative through some new tactical approach to their goal of driving the British fighters from the skies. Park was equal to every challenge.

Dowding's role was less spectacular. But he had laid the foundations of victory in his espousal of radar and the eight-gun fighter. He had made certain that there would be enough Spitfires and Hurricanes to fight the all-important battle by resisting the Cabinet when it was moved by the French pleas for more British fighter support on the Continent. At the crux of the battle Dowding rejected the proposals for massing the fighters from other groups on the airfields of No. 11 Group for reasons which appeared wise then and wise now. It is easy enough to second-guess when the battle is over and the other fellow has retreated. Dowding had to make his decisions in the heat of the conflict, unaware of the next German move, fighting the Luftwaffe with most of his force but keeping a protective cover over the coastal shipping and making plans to defeat the night attacks.

Finally, there are those intangible factors like morale that play so large a part in all human affairs. The best military history, Basil Liddell Hart once pointed out, would be one based on what actually went on in the minds of rival commanders during a battle. In this case we would want to know what passed through the minds of thousands of pilots, British and German, during those hours in the air. At the time no one in Fighter Command even considered the possibility of defeat. That confidence which the German pilots gave to their Fuehrer and their system, the British gave to their aircraft and their service. The professional pilots of the RAF's Fighter Command were relatively few in number. They all knew each other, knew their commanders, knew their service. When the command expanded after the beginning of the war they did their best, in an indirect, self-deprecatory way, to make the newcomers understand that there was no other service like it, that given the opportunity Fighter Command could blow any other air force out of the air. That's morale.

They were not concerned with anything but "our" war, by which they meant the daily encounters with the Luftwaffe. They seldom discussed the doings of the other services although once or twice I heard airmen, hearing about the army's protests over the supposed lack of air cover at Dunkirk, give it as their considered opinion that "the brown jobs," as they called the soldiers, "didn't understand what air fighting is all about" and would be better occupied "learning to fight the Jerries." They were apolitical. Churchill was regarded with some affection, not because of anything he said about them but because he impressed them as having seen when other politicians were blind. The influx of amateur officers, who talked often of the war and politics, rather shook the professionals. "Good fliers, but they *will* natter," a regular commented.

Only very occasionally would one of them, by a casual half sentence or a single word, indicate that he and his fellows understood that this harsh, dangerous life they were leading was also a fulfillment of all they had been trained to do, a repayment by them of a debt owed to their country. A good cause counts. Instinctively, without finding it necessary to read about Belsen or Buchenwald, they knew that theirs was a good cause. And around their airfields lay the soft, green countryside of England and when they rose with the sun to wait for the Germans they could see the gray, sprawling mass of London in all its massive dignity. They were not far from home, living amid alien surroundings, but among their own people. It was their war and they won it.

A number of people, British as well as German, have argued since the end of the war that the victory of Fighter Command was not quite the signal achievement it appeared to be when the war ended. The argument that the victory by day was one part of a wider battle is certainly a valid one. But I find it difficult to accept the reasoning of naval commentators who suggest that it was the presence of the Royal Navy rather than the defeat in the air that was the main reason for the postponement of the invasion. Had the air battle been won, as Goering intended it to be won, the Luftwaffe would have been strong enough to keep the fleet away from the invasion forces.

There were legends on the German side as well as the British. The most persistent of these is that Hitler and the High Command never intended to invade England and that the German forces approached the whole operation in an almost frivolous state of mind. This legend is akin to the familiar one that Hitler "allowed" the British to get away at Dunkirk. It is part of the mythology developed in Germany since the war, whose fundamental thesis is that Hitler, not the generals or the admirals, lost the war. Obviously this legend is of the greatest assistance in maintaining the German claims to military omniscience which were sadly damaged by 1945. If you are shopping for a job with the North Atlantic Treaty Organization, your chances of landing one are improved if you can assure the Supreme Commander that the German generals knew how to defeat the Russians but were prevented from doing so by Hitler.

The suggestion that the German government and its High Command never seriously contemplated the invasion of England is nonsense. They approached the operation with a good deal of reluctance. From start to finish Hitler pursued his strange illusions: one that the British would conveniently surrender and save him the trouble of invading; the other that a combination of bombing and U-boat warfare would force Britain out of the war, also obviating the necessity of invasion. But, although due weight must be given to the presence in Hitler's mind of these two illusions, the fact remains that he did issue Directive No. 16 ordering the preparation of an invasion and that up until the third week in September he was prepared to launch the invasion. Hitler not only set the Luftwaffe the task of driving the RAF from the skies in Directive No. 16. He also assigned to the airmen their task in the actual invasion: "in this operation elements of the Air Force will act as long-range artillery."

The opening of the night-bombing offensive against London is often considered as tacit recognition by the Germans that they could not launch the invasion. My conclusion is that the night raids meant only that the Luftwaffe was beaten in daylight. But let us suppose that the night bombing had achieved the success at which Hitler and Goering aimed. Suppose that mobs of fear-crazed Londoners had swept through the shattered capital, forcing the government to make peace; a picture, incidentally, that was only a degree worse than that purveyed to the world by Dr. Goebbels's word painters? Does anyone believe that Hitler would have held his hand? Of course not. He would have invaded then, just as he would have invaded had the Luftwaffe won the daylight battle and swept the RAF from the skies. The Germans failed. They do themselves and their dead little honor by pretending that it was all a monstrous bluff.

How, for instance, do they explain the very elaborate preparations made by the army, navy and air force in the summer of 1940? We have seen how the navy scoured Western Europe's ports and rivers to collect a fleet of barges, transports and tugs to convey the invading forces. It also assembled a strong force of destroyers and light naval craft to escort this rather unwieldy armada. At the outset thirteen of the best divisions of the German army were selected to make the initial landing. The number was later reduced to nine after the navy insisted that the larger force was beyond its capacity. And it is interesting to note that these divisions were still assigned to their invasion role more than a year after "Sea Lion" had been indefinitely postponed. For a bluff, the invasion was a long time dying. Once chosen, these troops were trained with great thoroughness. At the start their commanders may have been a bit daunted by the problems presented by a cross-Channel landing on a hostile coast. But as professional soldiers of experience and distinction they settled down to master the new techniques and to train their forces for the day. They not only thought they were going to invade, they thought they were going to conquer Britain. Long and elaborate plans were laid for maintaining the supply of the invading forces once they had won a foothold. Arrangements were made to clear Folkestone harbor—the Germans expected to take Folkestone with the first wave —and use it as the first supply port. A detailed plan for the administration of the conquered island was drawn up, including, incidentally, the arrest and transportation to the Continent of all males between the ages of seventeen and forty-five. Britain was to be divided into six "Military Economic Commands" to facilitate the organized looting of its economy.

The immediate pressure of invasion was relaxed as a result of the Luftwaffe's defeat. But the long-term threat of invasion to take advantage of the physical and moral disintegration of Britain under bombing remained. Nothing in war is black and white. But the claims made during and just after the war that the threat of invasion ended with the British victory on September 15 can hardly be reconciled with what the Germans were doing and thinking at the time. We know the form the German night offensive took: the prolonged bombing of London accompanied, from November onward, by very heavy attacks upon industrial centers in the provinces. Looking at the offensive from the German standpoint, it is easy to see the reasons for their optimism over the effect of the night bombing.

The air generals did not need Dr. Goebbels's propagandists to tell them that an urban population confined night after night to underground shelters ran a grave risk of widespread disease. The British were aware of this risk and surprised when no epidemics developed. Influenza and diphtheria were awaited with foreboding. Neither developed. Curiously the medical records show no drastic increase in tuberculosis or other respiratory diseases. The

Londoner, apparently, was physically as well as mentally tough.

The Germans managed to kill a great many Londoners during this period. The total casualties from bombing during the war were 112,932 of which 51,509 were killed and 61,423 were seriously wounded. The vast majority of these losses were sustained during the great German offensive of 1940–1941. But these figures were lower than those anticipated by the British government.

The offensive in the air, by day or night, failed to cripple the island's economy. This was a rude shock for the apostles of strategic bombing in the Luftwaffe. They had counted on a prolonged offensive gradually reducing to a trickle the planes, tanks, guns and other arms moving from industry to the British forces. There were some notable successes, at Coventry and at Southampton to name only two. But the attack failed for three reasons. First, the tonnage of bombs dropped was not heavy enough with the rather slapdash bombing techniques of those days to knock out industrial plants. Second, the Germans had not counted upon the spirit of the workers which brought them back into factories still burning to clean up the mess and restart production. Third, the Germans suffered in this sphere and elsewhere from the same failing; they were almost always reluctant to reinvest in success. They not only underestimated British morale, they underestimated the ability of modern industrial plants to withstand and survive the sort of attacks leveled by the Luftwaffe in 1940. Liverpool or Manchester or Cardiff would be bombed very heavily for two nights and left teetering on the edge of chaos. But the Germans would interpret the results as a knockout and select another target. Meanwhile the wounded city would patch up its industrial plants, restore public services, and get on with the war.

A series of spectacularly silly command decisions by Goering helped Fighter Command to win the day battle. Was the Reichsmarschall's conduct not equally at fault in the night offensive? One of the most intriguing "might have beens" of this period is what might have happened had the Luftwaffe maintained its attacks on London in strength instead of switching the great weight of the raids to provincial targets. There were plenty of people then who feared that if the Luftwaffe continued to attack on the scale of September, October and early November the Londoners would crack. They were not cowards or pessimists. Rather they took the rational view that, although the people might adapt themselves to a nightly diet of heavy bombing for a short period, the strain of these raids and the steady, visible disintegration of their city would ultimately prove too much for even their stout hearts.

Comparisons of the behavior of the Londoners during this period and that of the Berliners under the much heavier attacks that began, by day as well as by night, on the German capital late in 1943 show that the people of Berlin responded with a courage equal to that of the Londoners. But one difference in the psychological outlook of the two peoples should be noted. When the heavens opened upon Berlin the people understood, however dimly, that the people of London had endured a similar attack which from the doctored accounts in their newspapers had been equally heavy. When I first went to Berlin in 1945 an elderly German spinster told me that the Berliners, when the heavy attacks began, were determined to show that they were as brave and as resolute as the Londoners. They were.

In the autumn of 1940, however, the people of the British capital had no such example before them. No urban population had ever before been subjected to air attacks of this magnitude and duration. They were the guinea pigs for all the fine theories of strategic bombardment spun between the two wars by the air generals.

Nor were they buoyed during this period by clouds of lies about mysterious weapons that were soon to reduce Berlin to a shambles. Even the inflated figures of German losses by day were no longer much comfort. For the day battle was over and the Luftwaffe continued to bomb night after night. The Londoners were told with brutal frankness that the war situation was extremely bad. The threat of invasion still hung over Britain and the Prime Minister had coined the grim slogan "You can always take one with you." Morale and resistance flourish on hope. In the autumn of 1940 hope was one of the many items of military equipment that were very short in Britain.

These conditions magnify the heroism of the people of London and, indeed, of all the other cities scourged and blasted by the Germans. But they do not explain it.

One part of the explanation is obvious. The British people at this time were led by Winston Churchill, one of the greatest men the island had ever produced. Churchill's genius as a war leader was expressed in two different ways. His first and most important task was to formulate and express to the world the will of his countrymen. When on his eightieth birthday the old war horse, as Stalin once called him, was honored by the House of Lords and the House of Commons he asserted that in those stirring times it had been given to him to express the resolution of the British, to give the lion its roar. My own belief was then and is now that, far from expressing British feelings, Churchill taught the people what they should feel in this crisis. He made them conscious of the opportunity before them to demonstrate to the world that they were not defeatists, not afraid; that they intended to continue the battle. This was a political feat of the first magnitude.

It is not especially difficult to be bold and resolute when the enemy is far away across the seas and a strong army is interposed between him and your city. It is much different when the enemy is there, in the familiar sky, night after night. But the Prime Minister informed the people of Britain that these were not sad days, but great days. He taught them to be worthy of their past. He did not echo them. They echoed in a thousand different ways the matchless words at Westminster.

The second Churchillian attribute that was of the utmost importance to his countrymen during that dreary period was his willingness to goad and push innumerable government departments into action. Any long succession of defeats promotes inertia and by the autumn of 1940 the British people and government, with the exception of the day battle in the air, had known nothing but defeat since April. The Prime Minister knew this. He also knew the best methods of getting action from the vast machinery of the civil service. There poured from his desk at Downing Street a steady stream of memoranda designed to ease the lot of the people of London. After taking shelter in a tunnel at Margate during a German raid, Churchill concluded that something must be done for those thousands whom the bombs had left without their homes or shops. He dictated "a letter to the Chancellor of the Exchequer laying down the principle that all damage from the fire of the enemy must be a charge upon the State and compensation be paid in full and at once."

Other memoranda testify to his abiding interest in the welfare of the people of London:

How are you getting on with the comfort of the shelters in the winter—flooring, drainage and the like? What is being done to bring them inside the houses? I attach the greatest importance to gramophones and wireless in the shelters. How is that going forward? . . . The composition hat for air raids which Mr. Bevin is promoting seems to me of the utmost importance, and if it gives a measure of protection against falling splinters, etc., it should certainly be mass produced on a great scale, and eventually made a full issue . . . There are considerable complaints about the Post Office service during air raids. Perhaps you will give me a report on what you are doing. . . . Let me know what progress has been made in breaking up the queues and in bringing vehicles back into service. With the earlier blackout it must be very hard on many. . . . I understand that there is a serious shortage of accommodation for welfare services of all kinds to meet the needs of the homeless as well as of the evacuation schemes. . . . I have authorised the ringing of church bells on Christmas Day, as the imminence of invasion has greatly receded. . . . There must certainly be no relaxation of vigilance.

From these and other memoranda from that period there emerges a bigger man than the one seen by contemporary historians. Churchill was not concerned solely with vast strategic plans or with the composition of ringing speeches. He was concerned deeply with the day-to-day difficulties and annoyances that beset the people of Britain. Once when he began to cry after a group of recently bombed Londoners had given him an especially warm reception, a woman in the crowd said, "He cares." Indeed he did. Beneath the rolling periods of his oratory the people of Britain glimpsed the reality of his caring. In this worldly aristocrat they found a man who understood the daily hopes and fears of Everyman. They might detest his political past and resolve to bring his career as prime minister to an end at the next election. But in this period of stress he was the only man to lead them because in a mysterious way he became one with them. When during the Blitz someone said of Churchill, " 'E knows 'ow we feel" it jarred. How could the great man with his brandy and cigars, his strategic preoccupations, and his political combinations know how they felt? The oddest lesson of the period is that he did.

But the Prime Minister's leadership in a dark hour cannot wholly explain popular resistance. Neither his oratory nor his solicitude for the people he led would have mattered if the people themselves had been unresponsive. Why they responded as they did puzzled me then and puzzles me now. On the one hand there is a whole array of reasons: the British were a homogenous people proud of their past with a distinctly martial if not militarist character. But one can argue with equal justification that the lot of the poorer classes in Britain in the twenty-one years between the wars had been miserable, worse probably than that of their contemporaries in Germany. Yet it was the poor who withstood the bombing by day and by night and whose stubborn determination to live and work under the conditions imposed by the enemy provided the foundation for the physical effort of a nation in arms. The young pilots of Fighter Command were largely drawn from the middle class, the class which in many ways was more distant from the working class than the aristocrats symbolized by Churchill. Yet it was the partnership of these two classes, one in the clear sunlight against the bright blue of the summer skies and the other in the grimy streets and bustling factories, that proved unbeatable. Whatever it was that impelled the working people of Britain to stand by the state in its hour of greatest trial, a sense of history, national character, sheer bullheaded refusal to face the facts, it was enough to win. Is there a moral in this battle?

I think there is. And it is a moral that is not without application in our own time, one that we are apt to forget.

The moral is simply that in periods of great national peril a people accustomed to the democratic process are able to draw on sources of strength denied to a totalitarian regime. The Battle of Britain, as we have seen, surprised the world by demonstrating that a democracy could match and indeed overtake a totalitarian state in technical progress. This was an important lesson. But it is dwarfed by the effect of the performance of the people of Britain in 1940.

When that year dawned totalitarian systems were everywhere in the ascendant. Germany, Italy, Spain dominated Europe with their imitators developing in the Balkans. The most populous of all totalitarian tyrannies frowned westward from the Kremlin. The Japanese Empire overshadowed the East. When, after the terrible events of May and June, France fumbled toward a new form of government it bore the familiar fascist stigmata. Totalitarianism, a good many earnest, somewhat ingenuous Americans concluded, was the wave of the future. Democracy had been all very well for its time and its problems. But the time was different now in 1940 and the problems were different. "Look what Hitler has done for Germany," they said in the country clubs. "Terrible about the Jews, of course, but you can't make an omelette . . . Look at Mussolini in Italy. Done a hell of a lot for that country. Got rid of the beggars and the trains run on time. I tell you these people have got something." And as they marched imperiously into the future behind their bands and framed by their victorious banners, the dictators really did appear to have something.

Then finally the most powerful and ruthless of the dictatorships found itself face to face with its great enemy of this century. The Germans were sailing against England and the wind was fair. Over there behind the Channel and the Dover cliffs, the British behaved just as those critics of democracy and admirers of the efficient dictatorships might have expected. At almost exactly the moment when the German tide swept westward over Europe they elected to throw out one government and install another. They spent a great deal of time and effort debating whether they really had been right in locking up all those aliens. They continued, under the shadow of the most awful danger, to bicker among themselves, to make frivolous jokes about their own attempts to defend their island. "My God," men said in Washington, "can't they see what's going to happen? The old Hun will murder them. It's the end of the British Empire."

Then the storm broke and raged with unprecedented fury for five and one-half months. In January the smoke drifts away and the world peers at the battle. Do they find Hitler in Buckingham Palace and German soldiers marching through England's green and pleasant land? No, indeed. They find the British still there, shaken, tired and mourning their dead, but still there. And in the pale sunlight of January the fighter squadrons that sweep across the Channel are sweeping eastward, for Fighter Command has won the day.

This is the lesson 1940 teaches. Despite its fumbling and uncertainties, democracy by its representation of the mind and spirit of all the people can in hours of trial exhibit a resiliency and morale that can be shaken but cannot be broken. The bands, the banners, the clank and rumble of enormous armaments still existed east of the Channel. But now the German divisions were turning eastward, leaving the islanders alone with their dead and their glory.

The sentiments about authoritarian and totalitarian methods that were so fashionable twenty years ago are echoed today. "Of course," well-intentioned men in Washington say, "we don't want to become like the Commies. But we ought to have a little more control, we ought to be free from this eternal nagging in the newspapers, we ought to be allowed to direct the whole national effort. If we don't we'll lose to the Russians." The prospect is grim, if we think only of today and tomorrow. But the past counts too. Look back to 1940 and take heart. Democracy does the damnedest things.

These events took place only twenty years ago. But the pilots who survived are middle-aged men now, a little heavy around the middle, somewhat diffident in the day of supersonic flight about recalling their own experiences. Besides there are other things to think about: the new car to pay for and the next payment on the mortgage. The fitters and mechanics who sweated through the night getting damaged planes ready to fly again are foremen and heads of departments, good trade-union men, living in their council houses, cheering for Arsenal or Sheffield on Wednesday. The girls who with steady courage kept the machinery of the sector stations and headquarters running are mothers of families now. The old people who lived like troglodytes in the shelters are gone. To the survivors of the Blitz that second autumn of the war is a dark memory to be locked away at the back of the mind.

Inevitably a sight, a sound, even a smell unlocks memory's door. The pilots are young and slim and they stand on the edge of the airfield watching Y flight come circling in from patrol over Dungeness. The fitters watch from the hangar, counting the planes. "Lee, 'e's missing." " 'E'll be back, the sods can't get him." The mothers are girls again, grinning at the handsome, young flight lieutenant. "Ever so nice 'e was, polite and all when he asked for the gen."

> "But what good came of it at last?"
> Quoth little Peterkin.
> "Why, that I cannot tell," said he,
> "But 'twas a famous victory."

The poet's words suit cynics. The Battle of Britain *was* a famous victory. What came of it? Consider the shape of the world today if the battle had not been won. The figures of the battle recede again into time, the pilots and their girls and wives who waited and hoped, the mechanics and the fitters, the huge, foolish figure of Goering, Sperrle and Kesselring, Park and Dowding, the unknown thousands in the shelters who would not break, the German bomber crews who flew arrow-straight for London despite the winged death that tore at their formations, the soldiers at the antiaircraft guns, the workers in the factories, Churchill standing on an airfield watching the battle above.

> "Bless 'em all, bless 'em all
> The long and the short and the tall . . .
> You'll get no promotion, this side of the ocean
> So cheer up, my lads, bless 'em all."

[277]

Index

INDEX

INDEX

INDEX

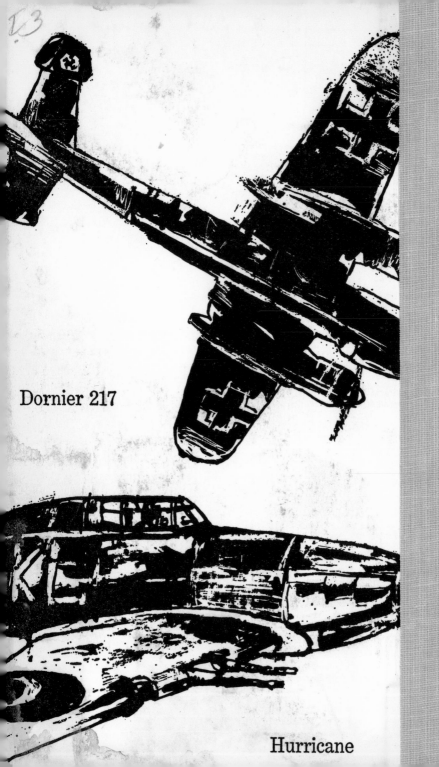

Dornier 217

Hurricane